ARA

y McAleavy

nities Inspector
oucestershire

CAMBRIDGE
UNIVERSITY PRESS

PUBLISHED BY THE PRESS SYNDICATE OF THE UNIVERSITY OF CAMBRIDGE
The Pitt Building, Trumpington Street, Cambridge, United Kingdom

CAMBRIDGE UNIVERSITY PRESS
The Edinburgh Building, Cambridge CB2 2RU, UK
40 West 20th Street, New York, NY 10011–4211, USA
477 Williamstown Road, Port Melbourne, VIC 3207, Australia
Ruiz de Alarcón 13, 28014 Madrid, Spain
Dock House, The Waterfront, Cape Town 8001, South Africa

http://www.cambridge.org

First published 1998
Third printing 2003

Produced by Gecko Limited, Bicester, Oxon

Printed in the United Kingdom at the University Press, Cambridge

Typeset in Monotype Octavian and FF Meta

A catalogue record for this book is available from the British Library

ISBN 0 521 62953 5 paperback

Picture research by:

Marilyn Rawlings

Sandie Huskinson-Rolfe of PHOTOSEEKERS

Illustrations by Jamie Sneddon

ACKNOWLEDGEMENTS
We are grateful to the following for permission to reproduce photographs:
Cover: (main picture) Popperfoto; (inset) Derek Hudson/Sygma
AKG London, 11(t), 39 (photo Associated Press); Camera Press, 13 (b) (IWM), 36 (r) (Choiniere), 61 (Braun);
Central Zionist Archives/Bridgeman Art Library, London, 47; Corbis Bettmann, 13 (t), 14, 16, 38, 52 (t & b),
53 (Reuters/Hershorn); Getty Images, 15, 19, 24, 37; Derek Hudson/Sygma, 54; Kunsthistorisches Museum,
Vienna/Bridgeman Art Library, London, 8; Mary Evans Picture Library, 9, 10, 11 (b); Hulton Getty Collection,
12 (r), 17 (Fox), 18 (Keystone), 21 23; Hutchison Library, 40 (t); Magnum Photos, 27 (Barbery), 30 (Bar Am),
33 (t) (Glinn), 43 (Bar Am), 46 (Steele-Perkins), 48 (Mayer), 50 (b) (Nachtwey); Popperfoto, 25, 35, 63 (United
Press International); Rex Features Limited, 41 (Torregano/Sipa), 45 (Photoreport), 56 (Sipa), 57 (t) (Daniel
Guelin-Sipa), 57 (b), 58 (Robert Trippett-Sipa); Frank Spooner Pictures, 44 (Gamma), 49 (b) (Gamma/Beitel),
62 (Gamma/Daher); Topham/Picturepoint, 5, 12 (l), 28, 32 (AP), 33 (b) (AP), 36 (l) (AP), 40 (b), 49 (t)
(AP/Miles), 50 (t) (AP), 51 (AP), 59 (AP)

Contents

The conflict today

One land – two people

At the heart of the Middle East is a small, disputed territory called Palestine or Israel. Two different peoples lay claim to it and have been in conflict for many years. They are the Jews and the Palestinians. Before 1948 the territory was generally known as Palestine; in that year much of the territory became part of a new Jewish state called Israel. At the time, both Jews and Palestinians lived in the area and Palestinians outnumbered Jews. In 1948 most Palestinians abandoned their homes and fled from the new state. Jews throughout the world were encouraged by the Israeli government to move to Israel. Since then the majority of people in Israel have been Jewish, and Jews have controlled the government of Israel.

The Palestinians who fled from Israel became refugees in neighbouring states and in the small area of Palestine that was not controlled by Israel. Many of these refugees, and their children and grandchildren, still live in refugee camps. A small minority of Palestinians stayed in Israel, although they were greatly outnumbered by Jews. In 1996, 18 per cent of the population of Israel was Palestinian and 82 per cent was Jewish. Palestinians in Israel say they are second-class citizens and are discriminated against in education, housing and jobs.

The Arab states

Israel is surrounded by Arab states – Egypt, Jordan, Syria and Lebanon. Many people in these states disapprove of Israel. Since 1948 most of the nearby Arab states have been involved in a series of wars against Israel. During the Six Day War of 1967, Israeli troops defeated the Arab armies and occupied those parts of Palestine that had remained outside Israeli control in 1948 – the eastern half of Jerusalem, the West Bank and the Gaza Strip. These areas had a large Palestinian population. Israel fought against Egypt and Syria in 1973 and invaded Lebanon in 1982. Egypt made peace with Israel in 1979. Jordan signed a peace treaty in 1994.

The settlements

Since 1967, thousands of Israeli settlers have gone to live in territories occupied during the Six Day War – east Jerusalem, Gaza and the West Bank. Settlers see themselves as completing the return of the Jewish people to the whole of the historic land of Israel. The Palestinians deeply resent the Jewish settlements and say that the settlers get an unfair share of land and water.

THE MIDDLE EAST

350,000 from Europe

283,000 from Middle East

264,000 from North Africa

Mediterranean Sea

Beirut • **LEBANON**

Tyre •   • Damascus

GOLAN HEIGHTS

• Haifa   **SYRIA**

Tel Aviv   Nablus •   **West Bank**

Jaffa •

Gaza •   • Jerusalem
         Hebron •

GAZA STRIP

ISRAEL

Jewish immigration 1948-64

Arab emigration 1948 (total 726,000)

EGYPT

Suez Canal

• Suez

SINAI PENINSULA

Gulf of Suez

JORDAN

SAUDI ARABIA

The establishment of Israel in 1948 led to the departure of most Arab Palestinians and the arrival of many Jewish immigrants.

The Holy Land

The early history of Israel/Palestine is closely connected to the birth of three of the world's most important religions — Judaism, Christianity and Islam. Religion plays a part in the conflict between Israelis and Palestinians. Jews are both a people and followers of the religion of Judaism. In practice, many Israeli Jews do not take religion very seriously, but for a large minority the Jewish faith is very important. Some religious Jews believe that they have a God-given duty to live where Jews lived in biblical times. About 10 per cent of Palestinians are Christians and the remainder are Muslims. Some Muslims believe that they have a sacred duty to fight against enemies of their faith.

The city of Jerusalem

The future of Jerusalem is a cause of bitter disagreement because both Jews and Palestinians see the city as their natural capital. The government of Israel has stated that it will never give up control of Jerusalem. Palestinian leaders insist that Jerusalem should be the capital of a Palestinian state.

The Dome of the Rock, the great mosque in Jerusalem, is the third most holy place in Islam. It stands on the rock where, according to tradition, Muhammad ascended to heaven. It is also holy to the Jews as the site of their ancient Temple which was destroyed by the Romans in AD 70.

Israeli political organisations

In the Israeli parliament (the Knesset) there are many different political parties with conflicting views. The two most powerful parties are Labour and Likud. The left-wing Labour Party dominated Israeli life between 1948 and 1977. Some leading members of Labour are prepared to compromise with Palestinians. Likud is a right-wing party. Members of Likud believe that Israel is entitled to take over all of the territory controlled by Jewish people in biblical times. The party takes a hardline attitude towards Palestinians.

The PLO

The most powerful Palestinian organisation is the PLO — the Palestine Liberation Organisation. Since 1969 its chairman has been Yasser Arafat. For many years, the PLO was banned in Israel and was involved in a violent struggle against Israel. In 1993, the Israeli government ended the ban and agreed to give the PLO limited power over aspects of life in Gaza and the West Bank. A new Palestinian Authority was set up to control day-to-day life in Gaza and much of the West Bank. Some Palestinians oppose the idea of compromise with Israel and are prepared to fight for an Islamic state in all of Israel/Palestine. These people are represented by an organisation known as Hamas.

The wider world and the Israeli–Palestinian conflict

There are about 10 million Jews living outside Israel. The largest and most powerful group of Jews lives in the USA. A result of this is that the government of the USA has had a big influence over events in the Middle East.

Until the collapse of the Soviet Union in 1991, its government also played an important part in the conflict. The Soviet Union provided many of the Arab states with arms for their struggle against Israel.

Israel and its neighbours

Lebanon

This Arab state is divided into Christian and Muslim areas. Since 1948 there have been large Palestinian refugee camps in Lebanon. PLO fighters were based in Lebanon from 1971 to 1982. They were forced to leave when Israel invaded Lebanon in 1982. The country was devastated by civil war between 1975 and 1991. The Syrian army finally brought the fighting to an end and now dominates politics in Lebanon. Since 1982, Israel and its Christian allies have controlled a small strip of southern Lebanon.

Syria

Syria has taken a leading part in the Arab struggle against Israel and the Syrian government claims that Palestine should be part of Greater Syria. The Syrian area known as the Golan Heights has been controlled by Israel since 1967. Unlike Egypt and Jordan the government of Syria has refused to make peace with Israel. Syria dominates the state of Lebanon. The president of Syria since 1970 has been Hafiz Assad. Assad supports factions in the PLO opposed to the leadership of Yasser Arafat.

Egypt

Between 1954 and 1970 Egypt was ruled by an Arab nationalist called Gamal Abdel Nasser. Under Nasser, Egypt was seen by many people as the leading Arab state. Nasser and the Egyptians were humiliated by the Israeli victory in 1967. Nasser's successor, Anwar Sadat, restored Egyptian pride during the Yom Kippur War of 1973. Sadat made peace with Israel in 1979. Egypt was criticised by most Arab states for this peace treaty. Sadat was assassinated in 1981 and replaced by General Mubarak. It was only in the late 1980s that Egypt was accepted back into the Arab community of nations. Some Islamic radicals in Egypt are still not happy with the government and the peace with Israel.

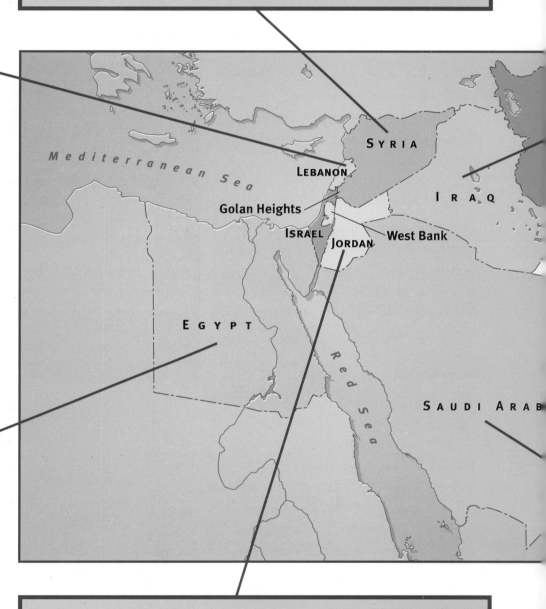

Jordan

Jordan was previously known as Transjordan. This state has a large Palestinian refugee population. Jordan controlled east Jerusalem and the West Bank between 1948 and 1967. These areas were conquered by Israel during the Six Day War of 1967. King Hussein has ruled Jordan since 1953. PLO fighters were based in Jordan from 1967 to 1971 but they were expelled because they threatened to overthrow the government of Jordan. King Hussein signed a peace treaty with Israel in 1994.

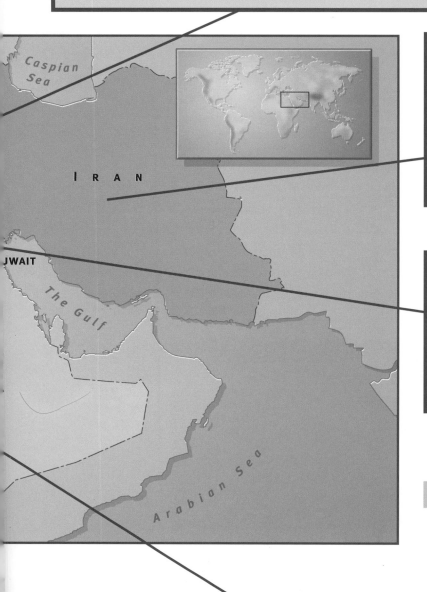

Iraq

Iraq does not have a border with Israel but the state has been heavily involved with Arab–Israeli politics. The Israelis bombed an Iraqi nuclear installation in 1981 to stop Iraq developing nuclear bombs. Under the leadership of Saddam Hussein, Iraq fought against Iran from 1980 to 1988 and invaded Kuwait in 1990. During the Gulf War of 1991, Iraq launched long-range missiles against Israeli cities. Many Palestinians supported Saddam Hussein during the Gulf War. Hussein was defeated and the Iraqis were forced to leave Kuwait.

Iran

Most Iranians are Muslims but they are not Arabs. Before 1979, Iran was a pro-Western monarchy and had good relations with Israel. During the revolution of 1979, the monarchy was overthrown and a radical Islamic government came to power. The new government was strongly opposed to Israel. The Iranian government encouraged radical Islamic fighters in other countries of the region.

Kuwait

This small oil-rich state provided employment for many Palestinians before the Gulf crisis of 1990–91. The war was caused by an Iraqi invasion of Kuwait. In 1990 there were 400,000 Palestinians in Kuwait. The PLO expressed solidarity with Iraq during the Gulf War and, as a result, most Palestinians were expelled from Kuwait.

Saudi Arabia

Saudi Arabia is a wealthy oil state. It is also the heartland of the Islamic faith and it contains the holy city of Mecca. Saudi Arabia provided financial support for Palestinians for many years but the Saudi government was angered by the way the PLO sided with Iraq during the Gulf War.

Discussion points

> Why has there been a long-standing conflict between Jews and Palestinians?

> What are the following organisations:
> > Likud
> > Hamas
> > Labour
> > the PLO?

> Which Arab states have made peace treaties with Israel?

Palestine and the Jews – from biblical to modern times

A God-given land?

The Jewish people played an important part in the history of Palestine for many centuries before the birth of Christ. The Jewish version of this period is told in the Bible. It describes how God chose the Jews as his special people and gave them the land of Israel. Under the kings David and Solomon, the Jews reached a peak of power in the 10th century before Christ. Some modern Israelis want the borders of Israel to be as they were in Solomon's day. After the age of Solomon, the Jews became divided and they were dominated by powerful neighbouring states.

A great scattering of Jewish people across the world took place under the Roman Empire. Rome took control of Palestine in 63 BC. Some Jews resented Roman control and there were two rebellions (AD 66–73 and 132–5). After the defeat of the second rebellion, Jews were ordered to leave Jerusalem and many were driven from the surrounding area of Judea. By the end of the second century AD Jews were no longer a majority in Palestine.

The emergence of two new religions – Christianity and Islam – was a further threat to the position of the Jewish people in Palestine. Jesus, who died in about AD 29, was a Jew, as were his first followers. In the seventh century, Palestine was conquered by the Arab followers of the Prophet Muhammad. They brought a new religion – Islam – and a new language – Arabic. Some Jews and Christians converted to Islam and intermarried with the Arab newcomers.

The Arab conquest led to the creation of the Arab Palestinian people. During the Middle Ages, Palestine had an Arabic-speaking Muslim majority. Palestinians today are proud of their own identity but also see themselves as part of a wider Arab nation. Most Palestinians are linked to other Arabs by a common belief in Islam. A small number of Christian Palestinians were not converted to Islam and there remains a Palestinian Christian minority today.

This 17th-century painting shows the destruction by the Romans of the Jewish temple in AD 70.

A persecuted people

Since Roman times, the Jewish people have been scattered all over the world. During the Middle Ages, the greatest concentration of Jewish people was in western Europe. The European Jews were repeatedly attacked by local Christians. Jews were expelled from England in 1290, from France in 1394 and from Spain in 1492. In response to these attacks, Jews moved either to the Islamic lands of north Africa and the Turkish Empire or to eastern Europe. By the beginning of the 19th century, a few Jews had returned to western Europe, but the greatest concentration of Jewish people was in territories controlled by the Russian tsar. Jews were required to live in a section of the Russian Empire known as the Pale of Settlement.

During the French Revolution, laws discriminating against Jews were abolished. In the 19th century, laws against Jews were scrapped in many other European countries. Some Jews tried to mix in, or assimilate, with their non-Jewish neighbours. In Britain one assimilated Jew, Benjamin Disraeli, became prime minister. Discrimination remained legal in the Russian Empire and many Jews began to move westward to escape poverty and persecution. While some Jews assimilated, others kept a distinct identity. Religious Jews continued to dream of returning to Palestine. They prayed that they might be able to meet together 'next year in Jerusalem'.

Arab Palestine

After the Arab conquest in the seventh century, Palestine was part of an enormous Islamic empire ruled, first from Damascus (in modern Syria), and then from Baghdad (in modern Iraq). Between the 12th and the 16th centuries, Palestine was controlled by Muslim rulers from Egypt, although Muslim power was interrupted by the arrival and temporary rule of west-European Christian crusaders. Control of Palestine changed hands once again in 1516 when the Turkish Ottoman family conquered the area. From 1516 until the First World War, the Turks remained the rulers of Palestine.

For many hundreds of years before the 20th century, there was only a very small Jewish population in Palestine. Historians estimate that there were about 25,000 Jews in Palestine in 1880; the greatest concentration was in Jerusalem. The great majority of their neighbours were Arab Palestinians.

Discussion points

> How did the Jewish people come to be a small minority in Palestine?

> How did Palestine become a largely Arab Muslim country?

The rise of Zionism

For nearly 2,000 years, Jews dreamt about returning to Palestine but most did little in practical terms to bring this about. This changed in the late 19th and early 20th centuries when many Jews became Zionists. As Zionists, they were committed to returning to Palestine.

Why did Zionism become such a powerful force?

By the early 19th century some European Jews no longer strictly followed the Jewish faith. They believed in 'assimilation' – the idea that Jews should try to blend in with the rest of society wherever they happened to live. They hoped that by living like their neighbours they would avoid 'anti-Semitism' (anti-Jewish prejudice and persecution). However, their belief in any real possibility of assimilation was dealt a great blow in the last 30 years of the 19th century as persecution of the Jews in several powerful European states greatly increased.

SOURCE A

This late 19th-century illustration shows a Jewish home being attacked near Novgorod in Russia.

PERSECUTION OF THE JEWS IN EUROPE

Germany

In the second half of the 19th century many Jews moved to Germany from the Russian Empire. They were viewed with hostility by much of the German population. Some German writers developed racist ideas about how the Jews were inferior to other Germans. In 1865 a writer called Eugen Dühring called for the extermination of the Jews.

Russia

In the late 19th century the greatest concentration of Jewish people was to be found in the Russian Empire. In 1881 the Russian ruler, Tsar Alexander II, was assassinated. The new tsar, Alexander III, was hostile towards Jewish people and many of his advisers were intensely anti-Semitic. In the following months there was extensive anti-Jewish violence, known in Russian as 'pogroms'. The government did very little to stop the violence, which continued until 1884.

Austria

Anti-Semitic ideas also flourished in Austria in the late 19th century. There was a large Jewish population in Vienna, the capital of Austria. In 1895 anti-Jewish politicians won control of the Vienna city council.

France

In 1886 a French writer called Edouard Drumont wrote a book entitled *The French Jew*, which was a vicious attack on French Jewish people. The popularity of anti-Semitic ideas is shown by the fact that the book was a huge best-seller. Anti-Semitic beliefs were particularly strong in the French army.

Searching for a place of refuge

The rise in persecution led many Jews to reject the idea of assimilation. Instead, they looked to escape from their European persecutors. Most of those who fled went to the USA. A much smaller number of Jews became attracted to Zionism. The Zionists believed that Jews would always be persecuted until they had a state of their own, and that the best place for this state was Palestine, their historic home. Zionism grew after the Russian pogrom of 1881. Between 1881 and 1891, about 10,000 Zionist settlers moved from Russian territories to Palestine.

SOURCE B

Ze'ev Dubnov, one of the first Zionists to reach Palestine, wrote this letter to his brother in November 1882.

My final purpose is to take possession in due course of Palestine and to restore to the Jews the political independence of which they have now been deprived for 2,000 years. Don't laugh, it is not a mirage. The means to achieve this purpose in Palestine could be to put all the land, all the industry, in the hands of the Jews. Furthermore, it will be necessary to teach the young people the use of arms. Then there will come that splendid day prophesied by Isaiah. Then the Jews, if necessary with arms in their hands, will publicly proclaim themselves master of their own ancient fatherland. It does not matter if that splendid day will only come in fifty years' time or more.

Herzl and the Dreyfus Affair

The level of anti-Jewish feeling in Europe was revealed in 1894 by what became known as the 'Dreyfus Affair' in France. Captain Alfred Dreyfus, a Jewish army officer, was accused of being a traitor. Dreyfus was found guilty on the basis of the false evidence of an anti-Semitic army officer. He was sentenced to life imprisonment in a French penal colony. Dreyfus was ritually humiliated by being publicly stripped of his officer's uniform and sword. The trial and humiliation of Dreyfus caused a sensation. To some Jewish people the Dreyfus case seemed proof that they were not welcome in Europe.

SOURCE C

To many Jews, including Herzl, the Dreyfus Affair showed that Jews would be persecuted unless they had their own state.

SOURCE D

Theodor Herzl.
> Why do you think he is a hero in modern Israel?

Theodor Herzl, an Austrian Jew, was present as a journalist at the humiliation of Dreyfus. The Dreyfus trial made a big impact on him. Within a few months he had written a book calling for the setting up of a Jewish state. Herzl was an impressive speaker and soon became a prominent leader of the Zionist movement. He organised the Zionist Congress in Basel, Switzerland, in 1897. This major conference involved representatives from 24 countries. The Congress received much publicity and was a significant milestone in the growth of Zionism.

SOURCE E

After the Basel Congress, Herzl made the following entry in his diary:

Were I to sum up the Basel Congress in a word – which I shall guard against pronouncing publicly – it would be this: 'At Basel I founded the Jewish state.' Perhaps in five years, but certainly in fifty, everyone will know it.

Herzl wanted to create a Jewish homeland virtually overnight. He spent much of his time trying to persuade powerful leaders to agree to Jewish control of part of Palestine. At the time, Palestine was ruled by the Turkish Ottoman Empire. Herzl attempted to convince the Ottomans and many other world leaders of the justice of the Zionist case. During his own lifetime, Herzl's methods were not successful, but after his death his dream became a reality.

Weizmann and Balfour

After Herzl's death in 1904, the leader of Zionism was Chaim Weizmann, a Russian-born Jew living in Britain. At first Weizmann made little progress. A major barrier to the success of Zionism was the fact that Palestine was under Turkish rule. The Turkish government was not interested in the idea of a Jewish state.

SOURCE F

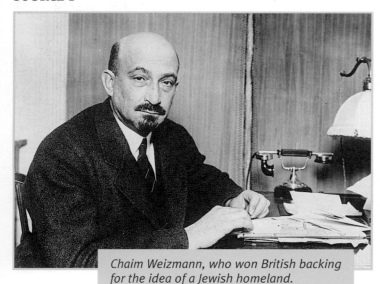

Chaim Weizmann, who won British backing for the idea of a Jewish homeland.

The Turkish Ottoman Empire fell apart during the First World War and Weizmann was presented with a great opportunity. The new power in the Middle East was Britain. If the Zionists could persuade the British to help, a Jewish state might be possible.

After many unsuccessful years, Weizmann eventually won British support. This success resulted from his friendship with the leading British politician, Arthur James Balfour. Weizmann met Balfour in 1906 and 1914 and impressed him with his case for a Jewish homeland.

The Sykes–Picot Plan

Although Balfour was sympathetic, he was not in the government, and government ministers did not take Zionism very seriously. In May 1916 the British and French governments produced a joint plan for the future of Palestine that did not involve any Jewish homeland. This was known as the Sykes–Picot Plan (named after two diplomats – Sir Mark Sykes and François Georges-Picot). Under the Sykes–Picot Plan, the Middle East was to be divided up into areas of distinct British and French control, with Britain in control of Palestine.

The Balfour Declaration

The political situation changed in December 1916 when Balfour became the British foreign minister. The Zionists now had a friend in the British government. Balfour persuaded the Cabinet to support Zionism. Most of his colleagues were unenthusiastic, but Balfour convinced them that it might help Britain to win the war. The Cabinet wanted to bring the Americans into the war and Balfour persuaded them that support for Zionism would go down well in the USA. The British government issued a statement supporting Zionism in a letter from Balfour to the leading British Jew, Lord Rothschild. The Balfour Declaration stopped short of calling for a Jewish state; it spoke in vaguer terms about the need for a Jewish 'national home' in Palestine. Despite this, the Declaration was a great triumph for Zionism.

SOURCE G

Arthur Balfour (on the right) in March 1917. As foreign secretary Balfour expressed support for Zionism.

SOURCE H

His Majesty's Government views with favour the establishment in Palestine of a national home for the Jewish people, and will use their best endeavours to facilitate the achievement of this object [they will try hard to make this happen], it being clearly understood that nothing shall be done which may prejudice the civil and religious rights of existing non-Jewish communities in Palestine, or the rights and political status enjoyed by Jews in other countries.

The Balfour Declaration, 2 November 1917

The British army in Palestine

The British army entered Jerusalem five weeks after the issuing of the Balfour Declaration. British control of Palestine was confirmed in the peace treaties that followed the end of the First World War. At the time, a League of Nations was set up to ensure world peace. The League authorised the British to continue to rule Palestine. (Officially Palestine was known as a 'mandated' territory because the League of Nations gave a 'mandate' or licence to Britain to govern the area.)

During the next decade, the British government allowed Jews from eastern Europe to enter Palestine. In 1918 there were over half a million Palestinians in the territory and 66,000 Jews. The number of Jewish immigrants gradually rose under British rule. Between 1919 and 1923 about 20,000 Jews entered Palestine. These new immigrants were, for the most part, committed Zionists and they played a major part in building up the Jewish community in Palestine. A bigger influx of Jewish migrants arrived in the period 1924–28. In 1925 alone, 33,000 Jews came to Palestine.

SOURCE J

Jewish immigrants arrive in Palestine in the 1920s.

Many of these migrants moved to the cities of Haifa, Jerusalem and the new Jewish city of Tel Aviv. The Jewish populations of Haifa and Jerusalem doubled in five years.

The British allowed the Jews of Palestine to set up organisations in order to administer the life of the growing Jewish community. These organisations were later to develop into the institutions of modern Israel. A Zionist Executive (later known as the Jewish Agency) was established as the highest authority in the Jewish community. Aspects of economic life were governed by the *Histadrut* – this was both a trade union organisation and the governing body for a large number of co-operative firms. Unofficially the Jews of Palestine were also permitted to set up an armed force known as the *Haganah*. The Haganah eventually evolved into the army of the new state of Israel.

SOURCE I

Two members of the British army in Palestine accepting the surrender of the mayor of Jerusalem in 1918.

The Arab reaction

Most Palestinians tended to see themselves as Muslims and members of a large family, rather than as members of a Palestinian nation. As a result, they did not organise for many years to resist the Jewish takeover. When they did come to believe that Zionism was a threat, they were much less successful than the Zionists in influencing the British government. Resistance was also weakened by divisions among the leaders of Palestinian society.

Anger at Jewish immigration was expressed through occasional violence. In 1921, fighting in Jaffa resulted in 200 Jewish and 120 Arab deaths. In 1929 there were attacks on Jews in a number of places — 133 Jews were killed, including 60 in the town of Hebron. To the Jews, the attacks were like the pogroms of Russia and they responded by arming themselves.

SOURCE K

A synagogue, damaged during the anti-Jewish rioting in Hebron in 1929. Many Jews were killed during the riots and Jews and Palestinians are still arguing about Hebron today.

The end of large-scale American immigration

In 1924, the government of the USA closed its frontiers to future large-scale immigration. Before this date, America had been by far the most popular destination for Jewish people looking for a new home. More than a million Jews emigrated to the USA between 1880 and 1914. Only 65,000 Jews moved to Palestine in the same period. After 1924, Palestine became the only possible destination for many Jews who wanted to escape persecution in Europe.

SOURCE L

A modern historian's view of the American government's decision in 1924:

This is one of the decisive events in the history of Zionism and the pre-history of Israel. Had those doors remained open, great numbers of European Jews would have found refuge in America between 1933 and 1941, and also after the Second World War. Immigration to Palestine in the same period would have been much less. The pressure towards the creation of the State of Israel would have been lessened.

Conor Cruise O'Brien, *The Siege*, 1986

>> Activity

1 Explain in your own words how each of the following factors contributed to the rise of Zionism:
   > persecution in Europe
   > the contribution of Herzl and Weizmann
   > the Balfour Declaration
   > the USA and immigration
   > the Arab reaction to Jewish immigration.

2 By 1930, Zionism was a powerful force in Palestine. What do you think was the most important cause of the rise of Zionism? Explain your answer.

Nazi Germany and the foundation of Israel

During the Second World War, German Nazis systematically murdered most European Jews. After the war the state of Israel was established.

Was the Holocaust the main cause of the creation of Israel?

People have interpreted the foundation of Israel in different ways. Some historians see the Nazi attack on European Jews as the most important cause. Many leading Israelis disagree and say that the single most important cause was the rise of Zionism in the 19th century.

Hitler, the leader of the Nazi Party, which was deeply anti-Semitic, came to power in Germany in 1933. The level of Jewish migration to Palestine reached new heights as Jews sought to escape from the Nazis. Between 1933 and 1936 170,000 new Jewish settlers went to Palestine. The Jewish population in Palestine almost doubled, reaching a total of 400,000.

SOURCE A

Jews being forced by Nazis to scrub the pavements in Vienna.

Focus

Look back at the last unit. Would it have been possible to create modern Israel without Zionism and the work of Herzl and Weizmann? Now look at the information in this unit and decide for yourself how important the Holocaust was in the making of Israel.

SOURCE B

The arrival of refugees from Hitler was vividly described by an English writer who was in Palestine at the time:

There was no more moving sight in those days than the arrival at Haifa or Jaffa of a Mediterranean ship carrying Jews from Europe: the spontaneous cries of joy at the first sight of the shore, the mass chanting of Hebrew hymns, the uncontrolled joy of these returning exiles (for so they thought of themselves). Palestine was the answer to Hitler! The Arabs looked on in dismay. Seen through Arab eyes, this great work of rescue and redemption had nothing beautiful about it and seemed to be an act of oppression against themselves.

Christopher Sykes in 1973, recalling Palestine in the 1930s

The Arab Revolt

The arrival of large numbers of Jewish immigrants sparked off an armed Arab uprising in May 1936 against the Jews and the British. Arab leaders demanded an end to Jewish immigration and Jewish land-purchase. Jewish farms were attacked. A guerrilla war developed between Arab fighters and the British army. By 1939, however, the Arab Revolt had been defeated by the British and the Arabs were disarmed. The failure of the revolt placed Palestinians in a much weaker position than the Jews. Unofficial Zionist armed forces remained ready to fight for a Jewish state.

The Holocaust – the British response

By 1939, the British government was against the idea of a Zionist state in Palestine. They put a strict limit on the level of Jewish immigration and continued with this policy even when Hitler began exterminating the Jews. In December 1941 the British refused to allow a refugee ship, the *Struma*, to land in Palestine. The *Struma* was cast adrift by the Turkish authorities and sank, killing 769 Jews. The policy of strictly limited immigration continued throughout the war. Some Zionists saw this as proof that Britain was no friend to the Jewish people.

After the war, a new Labour government took power in Britain. It was unsympathetic towards Zionism and blocked the mass immigration of Jews to Palestine. Foreign secretary, Ernest Bevin, wanted an independent Palestine in which Arabs and Jews would share power.

British refusal to allow the entry of Holocaust survivors was widely criticised, particularly in the USA. In July 1947, the British intercepted a ship called the *Exodus* carrying 4,000 Holocaust survivors. Three Jews were killed when the British stormed the ship. The remaining Jews were eventually forced to return to Germany. The treatment of the *Exodus* was condemned by many Americans. In July 1947, the British authorities executed three Irgun fighters. The Irgun responded by hanging two captured British sergeants. The killing of the sergeants led to an outbreak of undisciplined violence by British troops, in which five Jews were killed.

The Holocaust and American opinion

Before the war, many American Jews were suspicious of Zionism. They were afraid that a Jewish state would encourage people to say, 'We don't want you here, go and live in your own Jewish state'. The Holocaust convinced American Jews that there was a need for a haven for persecuted Jewish people. After the war, many Americans supported the state of Israel. This shift in American public opinion affected US politicians, who became increasingly sympathetic to Zionist ideas in order to win support from Jewish voters.

SOURCE H

This refugee ship, Theodor Herzl, *carrying Jewish immigrants, arrived in Palestine in April 1947. Two of the refugees were killed when a British naval party went on board the vessel. The banner held by the refugees states: 'The Germans destroyed our families and homes – don't you destroy our hopes'.*

SOURCE I

The American president, Harry S Truman, wrote to the King of Saudi Arabia on 25 October 1946:

The tragic situation of the surviving victims of Nazi persecution in Europe presents a problem of such magnitude that it cannot be ignored by people of good will. All of us have a common responsibility for working out a solution that would allow those poor unfortunates who must leave Europe to find new homes where they may dwell in peace and security. Many of these persons look to Palestine as a haven where they hope among people of their own faith to find refuge, to begin to lead peaceful and useful lives, and to assist in the further development of the Jewish National Home.

The British withdrawal and the UN partition plan

After the war, the British government found it difficult to pay for the troops needed to defend its worldwide empire. In Palestine, the Zionist campaign of violence added to the pressure on Britain to pull out. Britain announced in February 1947 that it would hand Palestine over to the United Nations. In May 1947, the United Nations set up a commission on the future of Palestine which produced a report calling for the partition – or division – of Palestine into a Jewish and an Arab state. On 29 November the General Assembly of the UN approved the partition plan. The Zionist leader, David Ben-Gurion, accepted partition but the Palestinians rejected the plan. They felt that it was wrong to give the Jews over half of the land when they were only a third of the population, and they did not like the idea that large numbers of Arabs would be ruled by the new Jewish government. In the following months there was increasing violence between Palestinians and Jews. Ben-Gurion held a ceremony on 14 May 1948 in which he proclaimed that the state of Israel was now in existence. The new state was immediately involved in a struggle for its life as it was attacked by Arab armies.

SOURCE J

The last British troops leave Palestine, May 1948. A huge vessel waits in the port of Haifa to take the men away from Palestine.

>> Activity

1 What did Hitler and the Nazis do to the Jews of Germany and Nazi-controlled Europe?

2 Why did the Mufti try to establish good relations with Hitler? What were the consequences of this relationship?

3 How did each of the following groups respond to Hitler's persecution of the Jews:

   > the British government

   > the Jews in Palestine

   > American Jews and the American government?

4 Look at the following sources:

   a What differences can you identify between the two interpretations?

   b Do you think that the Nazi attack on European Jews was an important cause of the creation of Palestine?

SOURCE K

There is a widespread belief that the calamity wrought by the Nazis in World War Two – the murder of six million Jews in Europe – brought the civilised world to vote for the establishment of a Jewish state. There can be no greater mistake. The destruction of six million Jews in Europe was the most dreadful blow to the Jewish state.

David Ben-Gurion, 1967

SOURCE L

Israel was born after the greatest catastrophe in Jewish history. But for Hitler, Israel could not have been born when and as it was.

Geoffrey Wheatcroft, *The Controversy of Zion*, 1996

The first Arab–Israeli War

Violence between Jews and Palestinians intensified during the last days of British rule. Much fighting took place on the Tel Aviv–Jerusalem Road. Arab forces repeatedly tried to control the road to cut off the Jews of Jerusalem from those of the coast. On 14 May 1948, when Ben-Gurion announced that Israel was in existence, the neighbouring Arab governments responded with war. Palestine was immediately invaded by 30,000 Arab soldiers. Although they outnumbered the Jews, the Arab forces were badly organised and their leaders distrusted each other. Officially, King Abdullah of Jordan had overall control, but in practice the other forces ignored him. Abdullah was keen to control Jerusalem and the West Bank. His forces fought hard for these areas but did little else. The Israelis resisted fiercely and survived the first Arab onslaught. They were greatly helped when the US and Soviet governments expressed support. On 11 June the UN arranged a month-long truce. This was a godsend for the beleaguered Israelis who then received vital supplies of arms. Fighting was renewed on 7 July and the Israelis captured the important towns of Lydda and Ramle. Ten days later a second truce began. This broke down in October when the Israelis attacked the Egyptian forces. Israel took the coastal strip between Tel Aviv and Gaza from the Egyptians and drove the Arab forces out of northern Palestine.

By early 1949, Israel controlled all of Palestine, except for two areas — the Gaza strip which was held by Egypt and the West Bank area, which was controlled by Jordan. The Arab armies were forced to admit defeat. On 24 February 1949, an armistice agreement was signed between Egypt and Israel. Further armistice agreements followed with the other states. The area controlled by the Jewish forces at the end of the fighting became the territory of the new state of Israel.

Map legend:
- Jewish territory under UN partition plan in 1947
- Arab territory under UN partition plan in 1947
- West Bank – became part of Jordan from April 1950
- Israeli border after 1948–9 war
- International territory

THE CONSEQUENCES OF THE ARAB–ISRAELI WAR, 1948–9

> A Jewish state was established within the territory controlled by the Jewish forces. Large numbers of Jewish migrants moved to the new state of Israel.

> Only the Gaza Strip, east Jerusalem and the West Bank remained outside Israeli control.

> The majority of Arab Palestinians fled from Israel and became refugees. A minority remained in the Jewish-controlled state.

> The governments of the Arab states were humiliated by their defeat. Arab leaders were discredited and lost power as a result. The government of Syria was overthrown in 1949; King Abdullah of Jordan was assassinated in 1951; King Farouk of Egypt lost power in 1952.

Discussion points

> Which side was more successful during the first Arab–Israeli War?

> What were the results of the war?

The origins of the Palestinian refugee problem

In 1947 there were about 900,000 Arab people within the region that came to be Israel. By the end of 1948, 700,000 had fled and had become refugees. Many of these people and their children have remained in refugee camps ever since.

Why did most Palestinians become refugees in 1948?

Zionism and the Palestinians

Most early Zionists had no intention of driving Arabs out of Palestine. They believed that there was room enough in Palestine for Arabs and Jews. Attitudes began to change as hostility grew between Jews and Palestinians during the 1920s and 1930s. The first prime minister of Israel, David Ben-Gurion, later said, 'I came here in 1906 and never had the slightest doubt that we could settle millions of Jews on both sides of the Jordan without dislodging one Arab, because less than ten per cent of the country was settled.' But, as prime minister, Ben-Gurion was himself a key player in the events that led to the flight of the Palestinian Arabs.

By the 1930s, Zionist leaders had begun to discuss privately the possibility of moving Arabs out of a new Jewish state. They were worried by the idea of a large Arab minority in the new country. The Zionist leaders hoped that an agreement could be reached with neighbouring Arab countries allowing for a peaceful 'transfer' of populations.

SOURCE A

David Ben-Gurion, the first prime minister of Israel. As a young man he believed that Jews and Arabs could live side by side.

>> Activity

Look at the following statements by Zionists about the Arab Palestinian people. What difference is there between the two sources? How can we explain this change of attitude?

SOURCE B

The absolute desire of the Jewish people is to live with the Arabs in conditions of unity and mutual honour and together with them to turn the mutual homeland into a flourishing land.

Resolution of the 12th Zionist Conference, 1921

SOURCE C

It must be clear that there is no room for both peoples in this country. If the Arabs leave the country, it will be broad and wide-open for us. If the Arabs stay, the country will remain narrow and miserable. The only solution is Israel without Arabs. There is no room for compromise on this point. There is no way besides transferring the Arabs from here to the neighbouring countries – to transfer them all, except maybe for Bethlehem, Nazareth and Old Jerusalem. We must not leave a single village, not a single tribe. And only with such a transfer will the country be able to absorb millions of our brothers, and the Jewish question shall be solved, once and for all.

Joseph Weitz, Director of the Jewish National Land Fund, December 1940

The start of the Palestinian flight

The departure of the Palestinians began in December 1947 during increased violence as both sides tried to seize land. In areas where Jews were strong, wealthier Palestinians often decided to move out. Between December 1947 and January 1948, richer Palestinians from Haifa and Jaffa left to escape from the fighting. Many educated Palestinians employed by the British left because they felt there was no future for them in a Jewish state. By the end of February 1948 about 70,000 wealthier Palestinians had left their homes. Their departure demoralised other Palestinians.

During March and April Jerusalem, and the roads that linked Jerusalem to the Jewish heartlands on the coast, were the focus for much of the violence between Jews and Arabs. At this stage many of the wealthier Palestinian families of the Jerusalem area began to move out.

SOURCE D

Khalil Sakakini was a writer and teacher living in the suburbs of Jerusalem. This is an extract from his diary from 30 March 1948:

The Jews launched a heavy attack on our neighbourhood last night. There were explosions, the like of which were never seen. The constant whistle of bullets and thunder of shells was worse than anything heard in previous wars. No wonder this situation has made residents consider moving to another neighbourhood. What was most distressing and nerve-racking was the anxiety which has overcome the women and children. Many residents of our neighbourhood have left for the Old City, Amman or Egypt.

Between December 1947 and March 1948 Palestinian villagers from places involved in fighting were sometimes driven out by Jewish forces, but villages where there was no fighting were left alone. Larger-scale movement of poorer country people began in March 1948. Fear of Jewish attack seems to have been the main motive. At this stage Jewish forces did not regularly force Palestinians to leave their villages.

A change of policy

The Haganah, the main Jewish armed force, began to change its approach to Arab villages from March 1948. At this point the situation was not looking good for the Jews. Arab attacks on the roads meant that the 100,000 Jews of Jerusalem were almost cut off from the Jews of the coastal plain. Many isolated Jewish settlements in the countryside were also surrounded. The threat of an invasion from surrounding Arab countries added to Jewish desperation. In this tense atmosphere, the Jewish leaders produced a new plan which stated that villages supporting the Arab forces needed to be disarmed or destroyed. It went on to say that each Arab village should be surrounded and searched. If there was armed resistance, the Palestinian fighters should be killed and the village destroyed. The plan also said that Arabs should be expelled from mixed areas of important towns. In April, the Haganah put this into practice and went on the offensive to get control of key roads. Some Arab villages near these roads were destroyed and the inhabitants were expelled.

On 9 April 1948 a joint force of hardline Irgun and Lehi fighters stormed the village of Deir Yassin, near Jerusalem. Over 250 villagers, many of them children, were put to death. Many of them were mutilated. This news sent a great shock wave through the wider Palestinian community. Many reacted to the news from Deir Yassin by deciding to leave their own villages.

SOURCE E

Khalad Hassan, a PLO leader, speaking in 1984 said:

Unless you are a Palestinian you cannot begin to understand how we felt after the massacre at Deir Yassin. Because of what happened there we really did believe we would all be killed when the Jewish forces entered our towns and cities.

After Deir Yassin, with Jewish forces close at hand, panic seized the Palestinian people in the big towns of Haifa and Jaffa. Between 22 and 30 April, about 60,000 Palestinians fled from Haifa as the town was taken by the Haganah, although there is no evidence that the Haganah commanders intended the people of Arab Haifa to leave. A few days after the Haganah attack on Haifa, the Irgun attacked Jaffa. By early May about 50,000 Palestinians had left Jaffa. During the months of April and May 1948, about 250,000 Arabs fled from their homes.

SOURCE F

A Palestinian woman and her children, living in a makeshift tent in the ruins of the Roman amphitheatre in Amman in 1949, over a year after thousands of Arabs fled from their homes in Haifa and Jaffa.

Arab encouragement?

Neighbouring Arab governments were unhappy at the news of the refugees because they feared that they would have to support them. The governments of Syria, Jordan and Lebanon tried to persuade people not to become refugees. By the middle of May the Lebanese government was blocking the border and not allowing refugees to pass.

>> Activity

Some people say that Palestinians were encouraged to leave by leading members of the Arab community. Look at the following sources. Do they support or contradict this theory?

SOURCE G

A Palestinian newspaper called As Sarikh *criticised refugees on 30 March 1948.*

The inhabitants of the large village of Sheikh Muwannis and of several other Arab villages in the neighbourhood of Tel Aviv have brought terrible disgrace upon all of us by quitting their villages bag and baggage. We cannot help comparing this disgraceful exodus with the firm stand of the Haganah in all localities in Arab territory.

SOURCE H

Syrian Radio was controlled by the Syrian government. It made this announcement on 5 May 1948:

Every Arab must defend his home and property. Those who leave their places will be punished and their homes will be destroyed.

The return of the refugees?

The flight of the Palestinian refugees created a new problem for the Jewish leaders – should they allow the refugees to return? In the middle of a battle for the survival of Israel, the Jewish leaders were not prepared to tolerate a Palestinian return. They felt that an influx of Palestinians would make the Jewish state less secure.

SOURCE I

At a Cabinet meeting on 16 June 1948, Ben-Gurion made his views on return clear:

I do not accept that we should encourage their return. I believe we should prevent their return. We must settle Jaffa. Jaffa will become a Jewish city. We must prevent at all costs their return.

Fighting broke out again from 9 to 18 July 1948 and a further 100,000 Palestinians left their homes. The pattern during this period is confused. In some places Palestinians were deliberately expelled by Israeli troops, in other areas Palestinians were left alone. The largely Christian Arab population of the Nazareth area was not expelled. However, in the Ramle–Lydda area nearly all Palestinians were forcibly moved out.

SOURCE J

Fighting began once again in October. During this phase of the fighting many of the Israeli commanders decided that Palestinians should be driven from the war zone. Between 100,000 and 150,000 refugees left their homes from October to November 1948.

After November 1948 the worst of the fighting was over. There were further small-scale expulsions after this date, but most of them were carried out by the Israelis as they sought to clear any Arab settlements that were close to the new borders of Israel. This was not carried out in a very thorough way and some Muslim villages remained near the borders. About another 25,000 people were made homeless by these operations.

Jewish settlement on Palestinian land

About 350 Arab villages were abandoned during the war. They were soon demolished and the process of setting up new Jewish settlements on the Palestinian land began almost immediately. By March 1949 there were 53 Jewish settlements, and between March and August 1949, a further 80 were established. New Jewish immigrants flooded into Israel throughout 1949 and many of them were resettled on the site of destroyed Arab villages. During the summer of 1949 immigrants moved into the village of Deir Yassin, site of the notorious massacre. The new Jewish settlement was known as Givat Shaul Bet. Other immigrants moved straight into abandoned Arab flats in towns such as Haifa and Jaffa. This process had gone so far by the middle of 1949, that the return of the Arab Palestinian people to their old homes had become unlikely.

Recent Jewish immigrants arriving in 1949 to build settlements on Palestinian land.

The Israeli view of the refugees

The following list is a summary of the official Israeli government view of the refugees.

> Israel did not create the problem. The war was started by the Arabs who ignored the UN plan to partition Palestine, and who invaded Israeli territory on 15 May 1948.

> Since 1948 many Jews have been forced to move from Arab countries to Israel. Between 1948 and 1972 nearly 600,000 Jews left their homes in Arab countries and emigrated to Israel. The greatest movement of people was from Morocco and Iraq – over 250,000 Moroccan Jews and about 130,000 Iraqi Jews moved to Israel. These people have been resettled and given new homes. Arab countries could have done the same for the Palestinians.

> The Arab leaders have deliberately kept the Palestinians living in squalor in refugee camps because this is good propaganda against Israel. Arab oil wealth could have been used long ago to solve the economic problems of the refugees.

SOURCE K

Palestinians living in refugee camps in 1949.

>> Activity

1 Since 1948 many people have been critical of the Israeli attitude to the refugees in the camps. The Israeli government, in turn, has vigorously defended its actions. Look at these statements by leading Israeli politicians. Who do they blame for the refugee problem?

SOURCE L

Golda Meir, later prime minister of Israel, speaking in 1962:

The Arab leaders exploit the Arab refugees for the purposes of their political war against us. We have accepted hundreds of thousands of Jewish refugees from Arab lands. Without waiting for compensation from the Arab governments for their abandoned property, we have done everything to absorb these Jewish refugees. The Arab leaders, however, do not look upon the refugees as human beings, but as one of their instruments of war against Israel.

SOURCE M

Yitzhak Shamir, formerly prime minister of Israel, writing in 1994:

Of all the sins committed by the Arab states against Israel, none has been more severe than that committed by these wealthiest of the world's nations against their own people. Not only did the Arab states refuse to absorb the Arabs who fled Palestine in 1948, but they kept them in the camps for 45 years solely for the anti-Israeli propaganda benefits to be derived from the sight of people living on inadequate charity. These are men, women and children, thousands of children, who could have been rescued from their dreadful lives by the investment of Arab oil revenues.

2 Critics of the Israeli government have claimed that the Jewish forces deliberately drove the Palestinians from their homes. Over the years the Israeli government has denied this and said that the Palestinians were not forced to leave but left because their leaders told them to do so. Do you agree with either of these interpretations? Using the information from this unit explain why you think the Palestinians became refugees.

The Palestinian refugees since 1948

After the fighting had finished, the United Nations tried to get the Palestinian refugees to return. The Israeli government refused to accept any returners. The foreign minister, Moshe Sharrett, said: 'They will not return. That is our policy. They are not returning.' Palestinians who did try to return were termed 'infiltrators'. Some of those who tried to return, attacked Jewish people. The Israeli forces viewed all infiltrators with great suspicion and hostility. Between 3,000 and 5,000 infiltrators were shot dead in the period 1949–56.

The refugees were eventually housed in makeshift camps in the countries to which they fled. From 1949 their basic needs were provided by a United Nations organisation known as the United Nations Relief Works Agency for Palestine (abbreviated as UNRWA). Many of the refugees have stayed in these camps ever since, and their children and grandchildren have grown up in the camps. UNRWA continues to provide basic services to the camps. In 1948 there were about 725,000 Palestinian refugees. Today the number has risen to about 3 million.

Those left behind

By 1949 most Palestinians had fled from Israel but about 160,000 remained. The new Israeli government imposed a strict system of military control on the remaining Palestinians until 1966. The Absentees' Property Law was passed in 1950. This officially confiscated any land or housing belonging to those who had fled. The government also took much of the land and property owned by the large Muslim charity known as the *waqf*.

In theory, Palestinians in Israel were given the same rights as Jewish Israelis. In practice, they were discriminated against in a number of ways. The Israeli constitution defined the country as the 'state of the Jewish people'. Palestinians were officially designated as 'non-Jews'. They found this insulting, because it seemed to imply that they were second-class citizens. Apart from members of the small Druze community, Palestinians were not allowed to join the army. (The Druze people belong to a religious sect that broke away from mainstream Islam in the Middle Ages.) Many jobs were advertised as suitable only for former soldiers, and this immediately ruled out most Palestinians.

ESTIMATED PALESTINIAN POPULATION, 1995

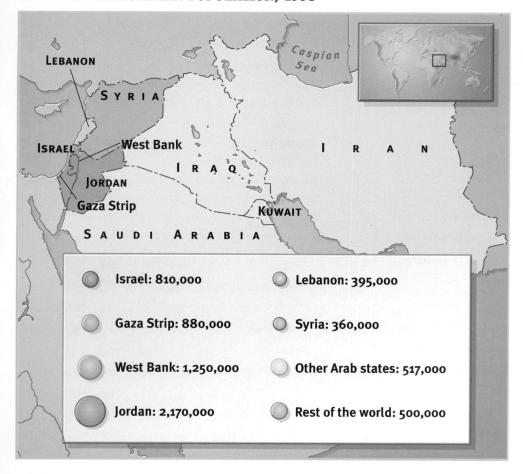

Israel: 810,000

Gaza Strip: 880,000

West Bank: 1,250,000

Jordan: 2,170,000

Lebanon: 395,000

Syria: 360,000

Other Arab states: 517,000

Rest of the world: 500,000

>> Activity

1 How did the government of Israel treat Palestinian refugees who wished to return?

2 How were the Palestinians who remained within Israel treated?

The Suez crisis and the Sinai campaign

An uneasy peace

There was no real peace in the Middle East after the events of 1948–9. Tension rose as a result of an arms deal between Czechoslovakia and Egypt in 1955. The Israelis saw the arms deal as the first step in a Soviet plot to support an Egyptian attack on Israel. Israeli fears grew when Egypt, Syria and Jordan joined together to plan military operations.

Nasser and Suez

While the government of Israel was increasingly anxious, Britain and France argued with Egypt over the Suez Canal. The Egyptian ruler, Nasser, was annoyed when the Americans and the British refused to supply him with arms. In July 1956 the US government withdrew its support for a massive engineering project at the Aswan Dam. Nasser responded by asking the Soviets for help and by seizing the Suez Canal from a company controlled by Britain and France.

The French and British governments decided to take back the Suez Canal by force. They secretly invited Israel to help overthrow Nasser. The plan was for Israel to invade Egypt. The French and British would pretend to be interested in separating the two sides and would send troops to the Canal. In the resulting turmoil Nasser would lose power.

The Israeli invasion of the Sinai

Israel invaded Egypt on 29 October 1956. At first the Israeli attack was extremely successful. They took large numbers of Egyptian prisoners and by 5 November were in control of the whole Sinai peninsula. The plan went wrong when British and French forces invaded. On 5 November British and French troops seized the mouth of the Suez Canal. There was widespread outrage at the news that these two European countries had invaded Egypt. Britain, France and Israel were condemned at the United Nations. The Americans were angered by the attack on Egypt and they refused to support their allies. Under a torrent of criticism, the plan to overturn Nasser fell apart. The British and the French withdrew.

Gamal Abdel Nasser.

Under American pressure, the Israelis reluctantly agreed to pull out of the Sinai and a United Nations force moved in to keep the two sides apart.

AFTER SUEZ

> The Egyptian leader, Nasser gained greatly in prestige for the way he had defied his enemies. He became a hero throughout the Arab world.

> The Soviet Union was admired by many radical Arabs for supporting Nasser. Soviet influence in the Arab world increased.

> Israel soon won back the support of the Americans. The Suez crisis became an isolated episode in the story of Israeli–American friendship.

> The success of the Israeli armed forces proved how formidable Israel was as an enemy. For several years after Suez no Arab countries were prepared to go to war against Israel.

Discussion points

> How successful was Israel during the Suez crisis?

> What were the consequences of the fighting in 1956?

The early days of the Israeli–Palestinian conflict

The birth of Zionism

Jewish and Palestinian people have lived in the area known as Palestine or Israel for thousands of years. During the time of the Roman Empire most Jews left Palestine and went to live elsewhere. Throughout the Middle Ages the majority of the population were Muslim Palestinians. In the late 19th century Jews were persecuted in several European countries. Some of these Jews decided to move to Palestine. They were called Zionists and they wanted to rebuild a Jewish homeland in the Middle East. The first great Zionist leader was Theodor Herzl (1860–1904). He campaigned unsuccessfully for a Jewish state.

British control

Turkish control of Palestine collapsed during the First World War and Britain took over. In 1917 the British government promised to establish a Jewish homeland in Palestine. This was called the Balfour Declaration (after British Foreign Secretary, Arthur Balfour). The British let many Jews move to Palestine in the 1920s. After 1933 many German Jews fled to Palestine to escape from persecution by Hitler. There was an armed Arab revolt between 1936 and 1939. The revolt was defeated but the British government became hostile towards Zionism.

After the Holocaust

During the Second World War (1939–45) about 6 million European Jews were murdered by Hitler and his Nazi followers. This atrocity is known as the Holocaust. The US government and the large American Jewish community became convinced that a Jewish state in Palestine was essential as a haven for Jewish people. After the war Jewish fighters clashed with the British forces because the British were reluctant to let many Jewish refugees into Palestine. In 1947 the British government announced its plan to pull out of Palestine and the United Nations decided that Palestine should be partitioned into a Jewish and a Palestinian state.

The birth of Israel

The Jewish state of Israel came into being in May 1948 as the British forces left Palestine. Arab armies immediately entered Palestine and fought with the Israeli forces. By early 1949 the Israelis had defeated the Arab forces and secured the existence of Israel. The two sides fought again in 1956 during the Suez crisis (known in Israel as the Sinai campaign). Once again the Israelis were victorious, although the Americans later forced them to withdraw from land seized from Egypt.

1967 – the Six Day War

In June 1967 the Israeli armed forces humiliated the neighbouring Arab states in the Six Day War. The Israelis occupied large areas of Egyptian, Jordanian and Syrian territory and large numbers of Palestinians came under Israeli control.

What were the causes and consequences of the Six Day War?

Focus

In 1994 a Jewish historian called Avi Shlaim commented on what he saw as the main cause of the 1967 war: 'The Six Day War resulted from brinkmanship by Nasser that went over the brink.' By this he meant that the Egyptian leader, Nasser did not want war, but caused the war by his aggressive statements and actions.

Look at the following information:

> What evidence can you find that Nasser caused the war?

> What evidence is there of other causes of the war?

> Do you agree with Shlaim that the actions of Nasser were the main cause of the war?

The Egyptian leader, Nasser, was a hero to most Arabs in the 1950s, but as time went on he faced a number of difficulties and his reputation declined. In 1958 Egypt and Syria officially merged together to form a new state called the United Arab Republic. Nasser claimed that this was the first step towards the unification of the whole Arab world and the destruction of Israel. But the link between Egypt and Syria was not successful. The Syrians objected to taking orders from Egypt and they eventually pulled out of the United Arab Republic in 1961, which made Nasser look foolish. In 1962 Egyptian troops became involved in a civil war in Yemen. Nasser hoped that his forces would swiftly bring the war in Yemen to an end but again his plans went wrong. The Egyptian troops were not able to win a swift victory and they became bogged down in prolonged fighting.

Nasser threatens war

By the mid-1960s many Arab leaders were publicly critical of Nasser. The Syrian leaders accused Nasser of cowardice in his attitude towards Israel. They tried to prove themselves to be the new leaders of the Arab world by taking an aggressive approach to the Israelis. In 1966 and early 1967 Syria allowed regular small-scale guerrilla attacks on Israel. This tough Syrian attitude put pressure on Nasser to prove that he was still determined to overthrow Israel. In 1967 he made increasingly threatening speeches in which he talked about the forthcoming extermination of Israel.

The tension mounts

Developments in Israeli politics led Nasser to imagine that he could threaten Israel without any danger of retaliation. Ben-Gurion, the tough Israeli leader, left office and argued with other members of the Labour Party. The new prime minister, Levi Eshkol, was seen as being much weaker than Ben-Gurion in his approach to defence. This encouraged Nasser to think that it was safe to threaten war against Israel because the weak new Israeli government would not respond.

In early May 1967, there was a high level of tension on the border between Israel and Syria. Clashes between Syria and Israel created a problem for Nasser. He felt that Israel might launch a full-scale war against Syria. He knew that Egypt was not ready for war but he was worried about his reputation. He was afraid that if he was not seen to be supporting Syria he would be despised by his fellow Arabs as a coward.

Nasser decided to increase his threats against Israel. By talking tough he hoped to stop Israel from attacking Syria. He calculated that Israel would not want war on two fronts.

COUNTDOWN TO WAR

> **15 May** Nasser sent combat troops into the Sinai peninsula close to the Israeli border.

> **18 May** Nasser demanded the withdrawal of the UN peacekeeping force that was positioned along the Egyptian–Israeli border. The UN force immediately withdrew.

> **22 May** Nasser closed the Gulf of Aqaba to Israeli ships.

On the same day as he closed the Gulf of Aqaba Nasser said, 'The Jews threaten war; we tell them: welcome. We are ready for war.' This was bluff. Publicly, the Israeli government called for the Egyptians to pull back. Privately, they decided to call Nasser's bluff by attacking Egypt.

SOURCE A

Yitzhak Rabin was the Israeli Chief of Staff during the 1967 war. In February 1968, after the war, he said:

I do not believe that Nasser wanted the war. The two divisions which he sent into Sinai would not have been enough to unleash an offensive against Israel. He knew it and we knew it.

American support

The behaviour of Nasser was not the only cause of the war. Two other factors were the determination of the Israeli government to fight and the attitude of the Americans. Israel depended on the USA and, before they went to war, the Israelis were anxious to make sure that the US government would not oppose military action. They had bitter memories of 1956 when victory in the Sinai had come to nothing because of American pressure to withdraw. The foreign minister, Abba Eban, went to Washington to explain the Israeli position. On 31 May Dean Rusk, the US secretary of state, said at a press conference, 'I don't think it's our business to restrain anyone'. This was the message the Israelis wanted to hear – the Americans would do nothing to stop an Israeli attack.

The Six Day War

The war began on the morning of 5 June 1967. The Israeli Air Force attacked and destroyed the Egyptian Air Force. The Egyptians were taken completely by surprise and their planes were destroyed on the ground before they could take off. The Jordanians and the Syrians joined the war on the side of Egypt on 5 June without knowing that their ally's airforce had been wiped out. The Israeli airforce turned on Jordan and Syria and destroyed their planes. Before the end of that first day's fighting, a total of 400 Arab planes had been destroyed while the Israelis had lost only 19 planes. The air attack was a devastating blow for Nasser and his allies. It gave Israel an overwhelming advantage over the Arab armies. Having gained complete air superiority, the Israeli ground forces rapidly conquered the whole of the Egyptian Sinai peninsula. The Israeli army battled with Jordanian forces around Jerusalem. On 7 June Israel took control of the Arab east of Jerusalem, which included the old city. For the first time in 2,000 years, all of Jerusalem was now under Jewish control. The whole of the West Bank, with its large Palestinian population, soon fell to the Israeli forces.

SOURCE B

Israeli tanks during the Six Day War.

The Israelis then turned their attention to the northern border. On 9 June the Israelis attacked Syrian positions on the Golan Heights. The fighting on the Heights was fierce but the Israelis were again victorious. On 10 June the Israelis agreed to a cease-fire and the Six Day War ended. The exact number of Arab casualties is not known but it was much higher than the total of 777 Israeli losses.

The war was a tremendous triumph for Israel. Before the war many Israelis had become frightened and pessimistic about the future. They were relieved and delighted by the success of their armed forces. The conquest of east Jerusalem was a source of great joy to most Jewish people. It contained the Western Wall, which was revered by Jews as the remains of the ancient Jewish Temple.

SOURCE C

In 1979 Yitzhak Rabin looked back to the conquest of east Jerusalem as the proudest moment of his life.

For years I secretly harboured the dream that I might play a part in restoring the Western Wall to the Jewish people. I knew that never again would I experience quite the same peak of elation.

THE SIX DAY WAR

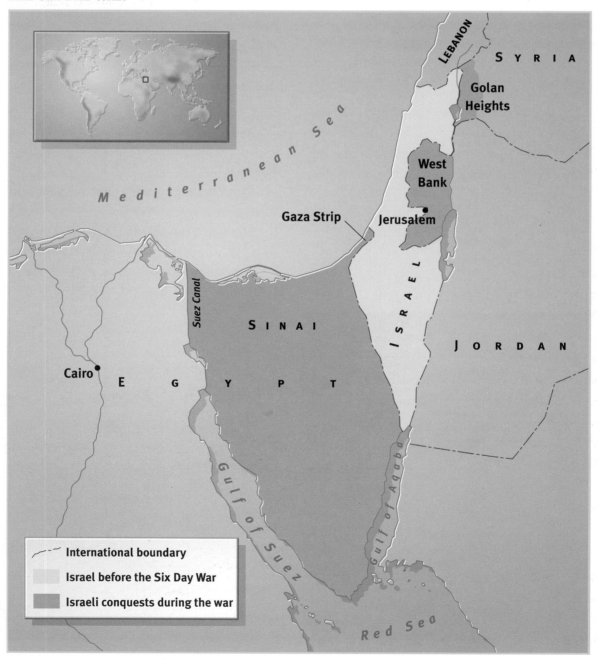

Legend:
- – · – International boundary
- Israel before the Six Day War
- Israeli conquests during the war

31

Resolution 242

After the 1967 war, many countries demanded that Israel should withdraw from the land occupied during the war. However, in contrast with the situation in 1956, the American government did not press for a rapid withdrawal. The United Nations Security Council met in November 1967 and agreed a new policy on the conflict. This was known as Resolution 242, and it stated two key principles:

1 that Israel should withdraw from the conquered territories;

2 that all the states involved should renounce war and recognise the right of all countries in the region to live in peace.

The two principles of Resolution 242 became linked together and known as the idea of 'land for peace' — Israel should withdraw from occupied land when her enemies made lasting peace.

The Arab reaction

After the Six Day War the Arab states were publicly defiant. Arab leaders rejected the idea of peace or negotiations with Israel. Despite this, the Arab governments were convinced that they could not defeat the Israelis through military force. As a result of the Israeli victories a further million Palestinians had come under Israeli rule. In addition, about 350,000 fled from the conquered territories and became refugees, mostly in Jordan. The defeat of 1967 led to a great change in the thinking of the Palestinian people.

SOURCE D

Yasser Arafat. The Six Day War contributed to the rise of Arafat as a Palestinian leader.

They decided that the Arab governments would never defeat Israel. They began to depend less on governments and began to develop their own organisations. This disillusionment led to a great rise in the influence and prestige of Fatah, the Palestinian organisation run by Yasser Arafat.

Israel and the occupied territories

The 1967 war created a great dilemma for the government of Israel — what should they do with the huge areas of territory they had taken in the Gaza Strip and the West Bank? Almost all Israelis agreed that, now that Jerusalem had been reunited under Israeli control, it should never again be divided. Israelis did not all agree about what to do with the other conquered territories. Some wanted to return the lands to Arab control in return for solemn promises of peace; other Israelis wanted to hold on to the conquered territories for ever. A month after the end of fighting, on 15 July, a Jewish settlement was established on the Golan Heights. It was the first of many settlements that Israelis set up on the land taken during the war.

SOURCE E

In September 1967 an organisation called 'The Land of Israel Movement' expressed the views of many hardline Israelis.

The whole of Eretz [the land of] Israel is now in the hands of the Jewish people. Our present borders guarantee security and peace and open up unprecedented vistas of national material and spiritual consolidation.

>> Activity

Explain in your own words how the Six Day War led to the following consequences:

> people began to call for a peace settlement based on the idea of 'land for peace'

> Arab governments became convinced that they could not destroy Israel

> the attitude of Palestinian people changed dramatically

> Israelis began to set up Jewish settlements in occupied territories.

Yom Kippur

War broke out again between Arabs and Israelis in October 1973. The conflict took place at the time of the Jewish festival of Yom Kippur. This war took the Israeli government and people by surprise.

Why did the Yom Kippur War take place?

In the aftermath of the 1967 war there was little progress towards a peaceful solution of the dispute between Israel and the Arab world. In 1969 the Egyptian army were ordered to use their artillery against Israeli forces close to the Suez Canal. The Israelis returned fire and there were regular artillery duels across the Canal. Israel escalated the conflict by mounting air raids deep into Egyptian territory. This was known as the War of Attrition. It finally ended in August 1970 when both sides agreed to a cease-fire. Shortly afterwards Nasser died and a new president, Anwar el-Sadat, came to power. Sadat was more prepared than Nasser to negotiate with the Israelis.

Sadat offers peace

Sadat was ready to make peace. He wanted Israel out of the Sinai and he wanted to reopen the Suez Canal. The closure of the Canal was a great blow to the Egyptian government because it lost the tolls and taxes from the shipping. In February 1971 Sadat made a speech

SOURCE A

Anwar el-Sadat.
> Why did he decide to attack Israel?

SOURCE B

Moshe Dayan. He was not interested in Sadat's offer of a peace deal.

making it clear that he was ready to make permanent peace with Israel in return for an Israeli withdrawal from Sinai. However, the Israeli government did not trust Sadat and was not ready for any compromise with Egypt. Moshe Dayan, the minister of defence, felt that Israel would remain strong if it held on to the land conquered in 1967. He repeatedly said, 'Israel has no foreign policy, only a defence policy'. This meant that Israel did not need to do deals with neighbouring countries as long as it had good borders and good armed forces. Dayan's views were shared by many ordinary Israelis.

Sadat opts for war

Sadat gradually came to believe that only by a display of military power, could the Israelis be forced to the conference table. Sadat built up the armed forces of Egypt with the help of massive aid from the Soviet Union. The Egyptian army was equipped with new powerful surface-to-air missiles, which made Sadat confident that there would be no repeat of the devastating Israeli air attacks of 1967. Sadat's view that there was a need for a war to end the stalemate was reinforced by a speech made by Dayan in April 1973. The Israeli defence minister said that the government now regarded the Suez Canal as part of the permanent borders of Israel.

>> Activity

1 Look back at the information on page 33. Explain in your own words why Sadat of Egypt decided to wage war against Israel.

2 Look at the following sources. What evidence is there in these statements that Israelis were becoming complacent in the years leading up to the 1973 war?

SOURCE C

An article from a leading Israeli newspaper, Ma'ariv, *on 13 July 1973 gives some sense of the complacency of many Israelis before the the Yom Kippur War.*

Our present defence lines give us a decisive advantage in the Arab–Israel balance of strength. There is no need to mobilise our forces every time we hear Arab threats, or when the enemy concentrates his forces along the cease-fire lines. Before the Six Day War, any movement of Egyptian forces into Sinai would compel Israel to mobilise reserves on a large scale.
Today there is no need for such mobilisation as long as Israel's defence line extends along the Suez Canal. The Arabs have little capacity for co-ordinating their military and political action. To this day they have not been able to make oil an effective political factor in their struggle with Israel. Renewal of hostilities is always a possibility, but Israel's military strength is sufficient to prevent the other side from gaining any military objective.

SOURCE D

The Israeli general, Ariel Sharon, speaking in September 1973 said:

There is no target between Baghdad and Khartoum, including Libya, that our army is unable to capture. With our present boundaries we have no security problems.

Attack at Yom Kippur

The war began on 6 October 1973. This day was a religious holiday in Israel, known as Yom Kippur. Simultaneously, Egyptian and Syrian forces launched a surprise attack on Israel. On the Suez Canal only about 400 Israeli troops and 30 tanks were in place. The Israeli soldiers were not full-time professionals, they were reservists from Jerusalem serving their annual army duty. The Egyptians launched a massive artillery attack on the Israeli positions near the Suez Canal. A few minutes later 8,000 Egyptian infantry soldiers attacked the Israeli defences. The Israelis were soon overrun. Israeli aircraft were shot down in large numbers by Egyptians using accurate Soviet missiles.

There was a similar Israeli collapse on the Syrian front. As in the Suez Canal area, the Israelis were completely unprepared and lacked the resources to stop the invasion. In the north the Israeli forces were greatly outnumbered. A total of 1,100 Syrian tanks faced only 157 Israeli tanks. The Syrian forces were soon within the Israeli borders.

The turning of the tide

In the first three days, the Israelis lost 50 aircraft and hundreds of tanks. After the initial shock they began a successful counter-attack. By 10 October the Syrians had been driven out of the territory occupied in the first days of the war. A day later the Israelis entered Syria itself. The Israeli position on the Golan Heights was re-established. The defeat of the Syrians enabled the Israelis to devote their resources to the Egyptian front. On 14 October an enormous tank battle took place in the Sinai desert. The Israelis won this battle decisively — Egypt lost over 260 tanks, while the Israelis lost only 10 tanks. The Israelis then moved on and crossed the Canal on 19 October. Soon the Egyptian Third Army was surrounded. Many leading Israelis wanted to push on and destroy the Egyptian forces. The American government put intense pressure on Israel, however, and the Israelis reluctantly agreed to a cease-fire on 26 October 1973. The Yom Kippur War was over.

THE YOM KIPPUR WAR

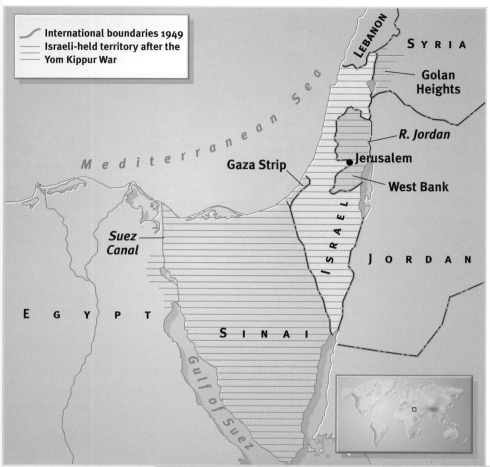

Legend:
- International boundaries 1949
- Israeli-held territory after the Yom Kippur War

Map labels: LEBANON, SYRIA, Golan Heights, R. Jordan, Jerusalem, West Bank, Gaza Strip, Mediterranean Sea, Suez Canal, EGYPT, SINAI, Gulf of Suez, ISRAEL, JORDAN

The aftermath of the war

The Yom Kippur War was another victory for the Israelis but the fact that they had been taken by surprise and had so much damage inflicted on them in the first part of the war had destroyed their reputation for invincibility. There had also been a change in world opinion between 1967 and 1973. At the time of the Six Day War much of the world was on the side of Israel. By 1973 there was much more sympathy for the Arab position.

During the war the rich Arab oil-producing countries placed a ban on supplying countries which helped Israel. After the war they also dramatically increased the price of oil. This encouraged many Western countries, particularly the USA, to look for ways of solving the political problems of the Middle East.

SOURCE E

Israelis, like these soldiers, were relieved at the end of the Yom Kippur War.

The Israeli reaction

Technically, the Israelis had won. Israeli forces were deep inside Egypt. The Golan Heights had been recaptured. However, there was no sense of victory in Israel. The mood was sombre – 2,500 Israeli soldiers had been killed in a war that had not been predicted. In the months that followed the war anger grew among Israelis about the way they had been caught unawares by the initial Arab attack in October 1973. The chief targets for popular anger were prime minister, Golda Meir, and her minister of defence, Moshe Dayan.

SOURCE F

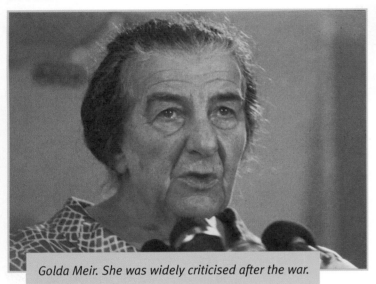

Golda Meir. She was widely criticised after the war.

After the war a government commission was set up to consider why the army had been so badly prepared at the start of the war. It was headed by a judge, Shimon Agranat. There was an explosion of anger when the Agranat Commission failed to blame Meir and Dayan. In April 1974 Meir and Dayan were forced to resign. Yitzhak Rabin became the new Labour Party prime minister. Although his government remained in power for three years it was the beginning of the end of the long years of continuous Labour control of Israel.

The USA and the Middle East

The war strengthened the position of the USA in the Middle East. It was the Americans who had brought the conflict to an end. For two years after the end of the war relations between Egypt and Israel were dominated by the figure of the American secretary of state, Henry Kissinger. He flew tirelessly from capital to capital in order to organise the gradual separation of the Israeli and Arab armies. This was known as Kissinger's 'shuttle diplomacy'.

SOURCE G

Henry Kissinger, surrounded by top Egyptian officials, at the Egyptian pyramids in November 1973. This picture was taken during a frenzied tour of world capitals which led to the signing of an Israeli–Egyptian truce.

Sadat hoped that the war would bring rapid progress towards a peace treaty between Egypt and Israel. While the war boosted Sadat's reputation it was to be several years before he secured a complete Israeli withdrawal from Egyptian territory. With the help of Kissinger he was able to sign two limited agreements with Israel in January 1974 and September 1975. The second agreement gave Egypt control of the oilfields of Sinai. Sadat continued his move away from the Soviet Union and towards the USA. One result was that in 1974 the USA began a programme of economic and military support for Egypt.

>> Activity

Did the Yom Kippur War strengthen or weaken the position of:

a the government of Israel

b the government of Egypt and the other Arab states?

The PLO

Since the late 1960s, Palestinian politics have been dominated by the Palestine Liberation Organisation and its leader, Yasser Arafat. At first the PLO was committed to the use of armed force and the complete destruction of Israel. By the late 1980s Arafat had moved away from the use of violence and accepted the existence of Israel.

How and why did the PLO change its policies?

Between 1948 and 1967 most Palestinians hoped that neighbouring Arab states would destroy the state of Israel. They were inspired by the rise to power of Nasser in Egypt and expected that he would lead an Arab army in a successful campaign to destroy Israeli power.

SOURCE A

Speaking in 1984 Khalad Hassan, a PLO leader, commented on Palestinian attitudes after 1948.

In those days we were under the impression that if only we could make the Arabs fight, really fight, Israel would be defeated. So immediately after the catastrophe [of 1948] we were dominated by one idea – we had to push the Arabs to another war.

The foundation of Fatah

As time passed without any progress some Palestinians gradually became disillusioned with the help they had received from the Arab states. They began to set up instead their own organisations devoted to defending Palestinian rights and fighting against Israel. One of the first of these Palestinian organisations pre-dated the PLO and was called Fatah. It was set up in 1959 by Palestinian exiles in Kuwait and its founding leader was a young engineer called Yasser Arafat. The word 'fatah' means 'conquest' in Arabic. Fatah developed into an active fighting force in the 1960s.

The PLO and 1967

The Arab governments set up an organisation to represent the Palestinian people in 1964 known as the PLO (the Palestine Liberation Organisation). At first the PLO was controlled by the Arab states, particularly the government of Nasser in Egypt. The defeat of the Arab armies during the Six Day War in 1967 was a great turning point for the Palestinians, after which the PLO became much more important.

SOURCE B

Young Palestinian fighters at the time of the Six Day War.

The PLO – a voice for the Palestinians

The events of 1967 led Palestinians to rethink completely their methods and their relationship with the wider Arab world. The Arab states, including Nasser's Egypt, had totally failed to defeat the Zionists of Israel. In 1968 Fatah fighters, assisted by the Jordanian army, resisted an Israeli attack at a village in Jordan called Karama. The success of Fatah at Karama encouraged more recruits. In 1969 the leaders of Fatah became dominant in the PLO and changed the nature of that organisation. No longer was the PLO a front organisation for the Arab governments; after the Fatah take-over it became an independent voice for the Palestinians themselves.

The PLO and Israel

The attitude of the PLO in its early days towards Israel was straightforward – the Jewish state had no right to exist and must be destroyed. The PLO believed that Jews whose families had arrived in Palestine since the First World War should be expelled. The founders of the PLO believed in the use of force against Israel. They wanted to set up an Arab state in the whole of Palestine. These views were stated in the Palestinian National Charter, a key document that set out the basic principles of the organisation. Originally written in 1964, the Charter was revised in 1968.

The structure of the PLO was very loose and this created many problems for Arafat. While his Fatah organisation was the single biggest group within it, there were several other organisations belonging to the PLO. Arafat did not control these smaller groups and they often pursued a different policy. The smaller organisations tended to be more hardline than Fatah, and most of them were based in Syria. They included:

> the PFLP (the Popular Front for the Liberation of Palestine) led by George Habash

> the PFLP–GC (the Popular Front for the Liberation of Palestine–General Command) led by Ahmad Jibril

> the DFLP (the Democratic Front for the Liberation of Palestine led by Naif Hawatmeh.

The armed struggle

Arafat had hoped in the aftermath of the Six Day War that his followers would be able to fight a successful guerrilla war against Israel. He was inspired by the way Algerian nationalists had driven the French out of Algeria through force. But the planned guerrilla war was not successful. The Israeli forces were too strong to be quickly dislodged by PLO fighters.

While the PLO continued to launch attacks on Israeli military targets from countries that bordered Israel, the organisation also began to use surprise attacks on Israeli civilians and other civilian targets. These acts were condemned by many as terrorism. While many of them were carried out by small splinter groups, all the main organisations within the PLO played some part. George Habash of the PFLP was unrepentant when accused of terrorism. In 1970 he said, 'We believe that to kill a Jew far away from the battlefield has more effect than killing a hundred of them in a battle: it attracts more attention.' In the same year his organisation gained massive publicity when it simultaneously hijacked and destroyed three airliners in Jordan.

SOURCE C

Clouds of smoke erupt from one of the airliners hijacked by the PLO in 1970. All three planes were eventually destroyed.

Munich, 1972

At the Olympic Games in 1972 a PLO group called Black September was responsible for the death of 11 Israeli athletes. In the same year 26 Israeli civilians were killed by Japanese supporters of the PFLP at Lod airport, in Israel. In 1976 a splinter group of the PFLP hijacked a French plane and took it to Entebbe in Uganda, where they held over 100 Jewish passengers as hostages. The Israeli armed forces flew 2,000 miles to Entebbe, killed the Palestinians and freed the hostages. After this, hijackings became less common but the use of violence against Israeli targets continued.

SOURCE D

Khalad Hassan, a leading member of the PLO explained the terror campaign in 1984:

Those of our Fatah colleagues who did turn to terror were not mindless criminals. They were fiercely dedicated nationalists who were doing their duty as they saw it. I have to say they were wrong, and did so at the time, but I have also to understand them. In their view, and in this they were right, the world was saying to us Palestinians, 'We don't give a damn about you, and we won't care until you are a threat to our interests.' In reply those in Fatah who turned to terror were saying, 'OK, world. We'll play the game by your rules. We'll make you care!' That doesn't justify what they did, but it does explain their thinking and their actions.

While many people condemned the PLO for its attacks on civilians, others admired the organisation for the way it resisted Israeli power. In 1974 the Arab League – the association of Arab states – declared the PLO to be the 'sole legitimate representative of the Palestinian people'. Arafat's position was strengthened in 1974 when he was invited to speak to the United Nations.

SOURCE E

Munich, 1972. Armed German policemen on the building in the Olympic village in which Palestinian fighters were holding Israeli competitors hostage. Eleven Israelis were killed.

Expulsion from Jordan

The rise of the PLO led to tension between the Palestinians and the Arab states where they were based. After 1967 Jordan became the main base for PLO operations. There was hostility between some of the Palestinians and the government of King Hussein of Jordan. The Palestinians disapproved of Hussein and wanted to topple him from power. Senior members of the Jordanian army were concerned that the PLO had become too powerful. Fierce fighting broke out between the PLO and the Jordanians in September 1970. The Palestinians called this period of fighting Black September, because of the heavy casualties they suffered. A cease-fire was eventually arranged. Fighting began again in 1971 and the Palestinian guerrillas were forced to leave Jordan.

SOURCE F

King Hussein of Jordan.

SOURCE G

The PLO in the Lebanon. Members of Fatah display pictures of their leader, Yasser Arafat, and the Ayatollah Khomeini, the Shia Muslim leader of Iran.

The PLO in the Lebanon

After their expulsion from Jordan, most of the PLO forces moved to Lebanon. From there, the PLO launched regular attacks on northern Israel. They also became deeply involved in Lebanese politics. Large parts of southern Lebanon came under PLO control. Lebanese society was divided and there was tension between the Christian and Muslim communities, and between rich and poor. The PLO sided with the poor Shia Muslims of southern Lebanon. When a civil war began in 1975 the PLO was drawn in on the side of these Shia Muslims.

Israel invaded Lebanon in June 1982 in order to destroy the PLO. The Israelis encountered fierce resistance but by August 1982 the PLO leaders were forced to leave Lebanon and moved to Tunisia, far away from Israel. Although the PLO had been accepted by much of the world as the voice of the Palestinian community, the use of force had brought little success in the struggle with Israel. Arafat's problems increased in 1983 when there was a rebellion within Fatah led by some hardline members. This failed but the rebellion was proof of divisions within the PLO.

Arafat chooses peace

After leaving Lebanon Arafat was forced to re-think his methods. He wanted a compromise with Israel. However, he had to be extremely cautious to avoid appearing to be a traitor to the Palestinian cause. Radical groups, encouraged by Syria, were ready to overthrow Arafat if he stepped too far out of line. The argument centred on whether to accept American demands that the PLO should:

> publicly reject the use of terrorism

> 'recognise' Israel, that is, accept that Israel was entitled to exist in peace within its pre-1967 boundaries

> accept the ideas behind UN Resolution 242, which stated that there could be an exchange of land in return for peace.

The powerful US government refused to deal with the PLO until it agreed to these conditions. In return for these concessions the PLO would be allowed to enter negotiations that might lead to Palestinian control of the West Bank and Gaza. Jordan attempted to act as a mediator in talks between the PLO and the USA between 1985 and 1986. This came to nothing because of divisions within the PLO.

In late 1987 Palestinian people in the West Bank and Gaza began an uprising against the Israelis known as the 'Intifada'. Young Palestinians challenged the Israeli forces with demonstrations and stone throwing. The Intifada convinced Arafat that the time was right for the PLO to take control of the West Bank and Gaza as a Palestinian mini-state. To achieve this he decided to accept publicly the American demands. He did this because the uprising made it look as if he was compromising from a position of strength and not weakness. In December 1988 Arafat finally publicly accepted the existence of Israel and the principle of Resolution 242. He also rejected the use of terrorism. The American government welcomed the statement and invited the PLO to talks.

For the PLO, recognising Israel and accepting UN Resolution 242 involved big concessions. The PLO had always claimed that it was entitled to control all of Israel/Palestine. In order to obtain the West Bank and Gaza, Arafat abandoned these claims and accepted the existence of the Jewish state of Israel.

Israel and Arafat

Some Israelis, including many members of the Labour Party, welcomed the change of PLO policy and saw it as an opportunity to make peace with the Palestinians. Others, including the Likud Party, distrusted the shift in policy and claimed that it was a trick. The Likud leaders claimed that the PLO had not really changed at all. They saw Arafat's announcement as a way of getting the West Bank and Gaza as the first step towards the destruction of Israel.

SOURCE H

The image of stone-throwing Palestinians confronting heavily armed Israeli soldiers became familiar during the Intifada and gained much sympathy for the Palestinians' cause world-wide.

Palestinian attitudes

Focus

Look at these sources. What do they tell us about changes in Palestinian policy since 1968?

SOURCE I

Extracts from the Palestinian National Charter, 1968:

> Palestine is the homeland of the Arab Palestinian people; it is an indivisible part of the Arab homeland, and the Palestinian people are an integral part of the Arab nation.

> Armed struggle is the only way to liberate Palestine.

> The liberation of Palestine is a national duty and aims at the elimination of Zionism in Palestine.

> The partition of Palestine in 1947 and the establishment of the state of Israel are entirely illegal, regardless of the passage of time.

> Judaism is a religion, not an independent nationality.

> The Arab Palestinian people reject all solutions except the total liberation of Palestine.

SOURCE J

We shall never stop until we can go back home and Israel is destroyed. The goal of our struggle is the end of Israel, and there can be no compromises or mediations. We don't want peace, we want victory. Peace for us means Israel's destruction, and nothing less.

Yasser Arafat, November 1974

SOURCE K

Our desire for peace is strategic and not a temporary tactic. We accept the right of all parties to exist in peace and security, including the State of Palestine, Israel, and other neighbours, in accordance with Resolution 242 . We totally and categorically reject all forms of terrorism, including individual, group and state terrorism.

Yasser Arafat, 14 December 1988

SOURCE L

Arafat turned his back on the PLO Charter when he agreed to recognize Israel. We stick to the original principles of Fatah. We are committed to continuing the armed struggle because we believe that Israel can never be a partner for peace. Arafat believes that he can achieve a political settlement and that requires us to abandon a part of Palestine. We believe that all of Palestine is the homeland of the Palestinians and we will never abandon it.

Abdul al-Nashash, a former member of Fatah, speaking in 1989

>> Activity

1 Why was it that for several years after 1948, Palestinians were not represented by their own organisation?

2 Explain in your own words how Fatah and the PLO were set up. Why did the PLO change after the 1967 war?

3 How did the PLO use violence to try to overthrow Israel?

4 Why were the PLO thrown out of Jordan in 1971 and Lebanon in 1982?

5 How and why did Arafat decide to change PLO policy in the 1980s?

Peace with Egypt, war in Lebanon

After 30 years of conflict, Egypt and Israel made peace in 1979. This was the result of an agreement between the Egyptian leader, Sadat, and the Israeli prime minister, Begin. Having made peace with Egypt, Israel went to war in Lebanon in 1982.

What were the results of the peace deal between Egypt and Israel?

In 1977 a new government came to power in Israel. Its leader was Menachem Begin, a man who had led the Israeli opposition for nearly 30 years. He was ready to make a deal with Egypt over the occupied Sinai desert. Begin was determined never to let go of the West Bank, which he believed should belong for all time to the Jewish people. However, he was ready to be more flexible about the occupied Sinai peninsula, because it was not part of the ancient land of Israel. 1977 was also the year when a new president took charge in the USA. President Jimmy Carter was very anxious to ensure a peace settlement in the Middle East.

Sadat in Jerusalem

The arrival of Begin and Carter offered the Egyptian president, Sadat, a further chance to seek peace with Israel, in exchange for the land of the Sinai peninsula. In November 1977 Sadat shocked the world – and horrified many Arabs – by announcing that he was prepared to go personally to the Israeli parliament, the Knesset, in order to seek peace. Begin accepted the offer and extended an official invitation to Sadat to visit Jerusalem. The Syrian leader, Assad, and the leader of the PLO, Arafat, were deeply unhappy at the way Sadat was seeking to do a deal with Israel. This did not stop Sadat from travelling to Jerusalem on 19 November 1977. The following day he spoke to the Knesset and called for a peaceful settlement of all the disagreements between Arabs, Palestinians and Jews.

SOURCE A

This picture was taken in November 1977 during the visit of President Sadat of Egypt to Israel. Sadat (centre) is seen conferring with the Israeli Prime Minister, Menachem Begin. Moshe Dayan sits on Sadat's right.

During the following months, detailed negotiations took place. They got bogged down over the future of Jewish settlements in the Sinai. Begin was prepared to pull out of Sinai but was reluctant to destroy these Jewish settlements. Sadat was determined that the settlements must go.

43

The Camp David Agreement

In September 1978 President Carter hosted a meeting of Sadat and Begin at his country house, Camp David. After 13 days of difficult negotiations the two sides reached an historic peace agreement. Egypt agreed to make peace with Israel; Israel would return Sinai to Egypt and close the Israeli settlements in the Sinai. Sadat and Begin also agreed to give 'autonomy' – by which they meant limited local powers – to the Palestinians in the West Bank and Gaza. The peace between Egypt and Israel brought to an end 30 years of conflict that had cost thousands of lives. The agreement over the future of the Palestinians was less impressive. It was rejected by the PLO and was never put into effect.

President Carter hoped that the Camp David Agreement would be the first step towards a complete Arab–Israeli peace. However, no other Arab states were prepared to make peace with Israel. Within days of Sadat's visit to Jerusalem, Arab leaders met in Libya and denounced Sadat. Egypt was isolated for years afterwards as other Arab states showed their displeasure at Sadat's 'go-it-alone' policy. Sadat himself paid a heavy price for his peace policy. In October 1981 he was assassinated by Egyptian soldiers during a military parade. His killers believed that Sadat had disgraced Islam by his deal with the Israelis.

SOURCE B

Carter, Begin and Sadat sign the agreements reached at Camp David in 1978.

Begin expands the West Bank settlements

Having achieved peace with Egypt, Begin was free to act elsewhere without fear of Egyptian attack. In six years he increased the number of Jewish settlements on the West Bank from 45 to 112. Begin also ensured that Palestinian opposition on the West Bank was put down with great firmness.

The invasion of Lebanon

After Camp David, Begin was free to attack the PLO in Lebanon, without risking war with Egypt. The Israelis had been concerned about Lebanon ever since the PLO leadership moved to Beirut in 1971. They were also unhappy at the growing power of the Syrians in Lebanon. In 1975 the Israeli government set up the South Lebanon Army (SLA). Its members were Lebanese Christians whom Israel saw as allies against the PLO and Syrian forces.

In March 1978, Israel invaded southern Lebanon. This followed a PLO attack on an Israeli bus from Lebanon which killed 34 Israelis. A large number of Palestinians and Lebanese were killed during the invasion. The Israelis withdrew from much of the country in June but kept control of a strip of territory close to the border.

Tension between Israel and the PLO in Lebanon continued after 1978. Israel invaded Lebanon for a second time in June 1982 with the intention of destroying the PLO and reducing Syria's power. They intended to set up a friendly government in Lebanon run by Lebanese Christians. The official Israeli name for the invasion was 'Operation Peace for Galilee'. (Galilee is an area in the north of Israel.)

SOURCE C

Israeli tanks overlooking the Lebanese capital, Beirut in June 1982.

SOURCE E

Two historians discussed the impact of the Sadat–Begin negotiations on the Lebanon:

On 9 November 1977 President Sadat of Egypt announced his intention to travel to Jerusalem to initiate direct peace negotiations with Israel. Israel was now free to take whatever action it liked in Lebanon. Sadat himself remarked in November 1977 that 'blood will flow in Lebanon and Syria'.

Peter Sluglett and Marion Farouk-Sluglett, *The Times Guide to the Middle East*, 1991

The invasion was intended to be very quick. In fact, it was three years before the last Israelis were able to withdraw from Lebanon. Resistance was fierce and the siege of Beirut lasted three months. Arafat and the PLO leaders finally pulled out of Lebanon in August. They moved far away to Tunisia. While they forced the PLO leaders out, the Israeli forces were unable to impose a Christian government on Lebanon. By the end of the war the power of Syria was greater than ever. About 19,000 Palestinians and Lebanese people (the majority were civilians) and 700 Israeli soldiers were killed. The Israeli invasion was widely condemned in much of the world and caused deep unease among many of the Jews of Israel.

SOURCE D

Abba Eban, a former Israeli foreign minister, wrote in 1992:

The position of the Palestinians in the West Bank became progressively worse after Camp David. Detention centres were established in Israel. Thousands of detainees were arrested without charge. Many of them were teenagers.

SOURCE F

A British newspaper described the killing of Sadat:

Camp David Killed Sadat

The version thundered out in the headlines of most Arabic newspapers and radio broadcasts last week, was that Sadat was doomed from the moment he went to Jerusalem in November 1977, and announced that he was ready to recognize the existence of the State of Israel. By that one act, committed in the third most holy city of Islam, he branded himself a traitor to his own religion and invited the 'execution' that finally came from the guns of his own soldiers.

The Sunday Times, 11 October 1981

>> Activity

1 What were the causes and consequences of the Camp David Agreement?

2 Look at Sources D–F. What can we learn from these sources about the consequences of the Egyptian–Israeli peace deal?

Massacre in the refugee camps

Worldwide criticism of the Israeli invasion of Lebanon reached a new level after 16 September 1982 when Christian fighters entered two Palestinian refugee camps and massacred over a thousand Palestinian men, women and children. The camps were known as Sabra and Shatila. The killings were carried out by Lebanese Christians but the Israeli forces were near at hand and did nothing to prevent the massacre. The war and the massacres led to a heated debate within Israel. During previous wars Israelis had united in support of their soldiers. This time many Israelis openly criticised the action of their forces. When people heard about the Sabra–Shatila massacres there was a peace demonstration of about 250,000 Israelis in Tel Aviv.

SOURCE G

The aftermath of the massacre at Shatila, September 1982.

The worst of the fighting was over by late 1982. The Israelis left Lebanon in 1985 but retained control of a so-called security zone near the border. The prime minister, Menachem Begin, was deeply upset at reactions to the events in Lebanon. He retired from the post of prime minister in 1983 and went into seclusion, refusing to talk in public about politics until his death in 1992.

Different views of the Israeli action in Lebanon

SOURCE H

Some Israelis were deeply critical of the war in Lebanon and the leadership of defence minister, Ariel Sharon:

Born of the ambition of one wilful and reckless man, Israel's 1982 invasion of Lebanon was anchored in delusion and bound to end in calamity. For meagre gains Israel paid an enormous price. It cost the Israeli Defence Forces the lives of 650 of its finest men. There is no consolation for this costly senseless war.

Zeev Schiff and Ehud Ya'ari, 1984

SOURCE I

Some Israelis believe that the invasion of Lebanon was justified. Binyamin Netanyahu, who became prime minister of Israel in 1996, speaking in 1993:

Much maligned at the time, Operation Peace for Galilee lived up to its name. Since the PLO's expulsion from Beirut in 1982 and the establishment of the security zone in the south of Lebanon, there have hardly been any successful terrorist penetrations from southern Lebanon into the north of Israel.

>> Activity

1 The Israeli invasion of Lebanon had a number of aims:
   > the destruction of the PLO presence in Lebanon;
   > the reduction of the power of Syria;
   > the setting up of a Lebanese Christian government that would be friendly towards Israel.

   Using information from this unit explain how successful the Israeli invasion of Lebanon in 1982 was.

2 Look at Sources H and I. What difference is there between these two interpretations of the war in Lebanon? Both sources are written by Jewish Israelis; how do you think different interpretations like this can come about?

Israel – a divided society?

Israel is a small country. The Jewish population is less than 5 million people. Although the number of Israeli Jews is small, they have many different views of how their country should be run.

How united are the Jewish people of Israel?

DIVISIONS IN JEWISH SOCIETY

> Religious Jews | Those Jews who pay little attention to the Jewish faith

> Israeli Jews from a European background | Israeli Jews from an African or Asian background

> Supporters of the left-wing Labour Party | Supporters of the right-wing Likud

> Israeli Jews who want to compromise with Palestinians | Israeli Jews who want the government to take a tough line with Palestinians

Zionism and socialism

During the early 1920s there were differences of opinion among the Jews in Palestine about dealing with their Arab neighbours. At first the dominant group among the Jewish community were left-wing socialists. The modern Labour Party sees itself as continuing the work of these early socialists. When they arrived in Palestine most socialist Jews wanted to have good relations with the Arabs. Other Jews wanted nothing to do with them and believed that force would be necessary to keep the Arabs from destroying Zionism. One of the earliest and most influential hardliners was Vladimir Jabotinsky. The modern Likud Party see Jabotinsky as their inspiration.

SOURCE A

Statements made by Jabotinsky in the early 1920s:

What is needed is an iron wall of armed force. The Arab has to be made to say to himself: 'Here stands an iron wall; the Jews are coming and will keep on coming; we are unable to prevent this; we cannot kill them.'

Every people has fought immigration and settlement by foreigners. There was no misunderstanding between Jew and Arab, but a natural conflict. No agreement was possible with the Palestinian Arab; they would accept Zionism only when they found themselves up against an iron wall.

SOURCE B

A socialist poster from the 1930s contrasts the honest left-wing worker with the idle right-wing rich man.

The divisions within the Jewish community increased after the riots of 1929. In 1931 followers of Jabotinsky left the main Jewish militia, the Haganah, and founded a new militant defence force, the Irgun. These people were also known as 'revisionists'. Socialist Zionists were not pacifists: they were prepared to use force to defend themselves. However, Ben-Gurion, the socialist leader, disagreed with the hardline approach of Jabotinsky. He called for *Havlaga*, a Hebrew term meaning self-restraint.

47

The impact of religion

Differences between religious and non-religious, or secular, Jews go back to the days before Israel existed. The pioneers of Zionism were not religious. Many religious, or Orthodox, Jews disapproved of the idea of non-religious Jews setting up a Jewish state in Israel. Today disagreements between religious and non-religious Jews are common in Israel. The education system is divided into non-religious and religious schools — about a third of Jewish children go to religious schools. Religious Jews also have their own political parties, the largest being the National Religious Party. The strength of these parties has increased recently. In May 1996 a record 24 representatives of religious parties were elected to the Israeli Knesset. The election system in Israel means that the big parties — Labour and Likud — usually need the support of the religious parties to form a government. The National Religious Party was allied to Labour for much of the period 1948–77. In the 1970s the party changed and became associated with the settlement movement in the West Bank. The National Religious Party withdrew its support for Labour in 1977 and this helped the Likud to come to power.

The settlement movement

For many Orthodox Jews the establishment of Israel is part of God's plans. They believe that the return of the exiled Jewish people to

SOURCE G

Religion is important for some, but not all, Israelis. Here soldiers pray at the Wailing Wall beside Orthodox Jews.

SOURCE H

Yitzhak Shamir. As Likud prime minister he supported Jewish settlers on the West Bank.

Israel is the beginning of the end of the world as we have known it. A new age of redemption is dawning. The capture of all Jerusalem in 1967 was an important step in God's plan. The next move is for Jews to settle throughout the ancient Jewish lands. For this reason many religious Jews are enthusiastic supporters of Jewish settlement throughout the West Bank.

In 1974 religious Jews set up a new organisation committed to settlement in the occupied territories. This was called, in Hebrew, Gush Emunim (which means the Bloc of the Faithful). Many leading members of Likud are not religious but they have supported the work of Gush Emunim.

SOURCE I

Yitzhak Shamir was Likud prime minister until 1992. In 1994 he praised members of Gush Emunim.

They are men and women of courage, intensity and determination who practise what they preach; who went, despite the difficulties and danger, to make their homes in Judea and Samaria (the West Bank). They are also deeply believing Jews: this, to them, is literally the Holy Land and it is God's will for them to settle where they do. I have always admired them.

Settlements on the West Bank

After 1967 the Labour government established a small number of Israeli settlements in the West Bank for defensive reasons. Likud wanted more settlements — many in Likud wanted to annex the whole territory. There was a huge expansion of settlements after Likud came to power in 1977. Between 1976 and 1996 the number of settlers went from less than 4,000 to well over 100,000. By the middle of the 1990s settlers constituted about 10 per cent of the population of the West Bank. When Likud returned to power in 1996 the government's first act was to expand Jewish settlements.

Tension between Palestinians and settlers has been particularly acute in the large West Bank town of Hebron. There is a large Jewish settlement outside the city called Kiryat Arba. In addition, about 400 Jewish settlers live right in the centre of a town of over 100,000 Palestinian Arabs. The settlers are protected by armed Israeli soldiers. In 1994 a Jewish extremist from Kiryat Arba killed 29 Palestinians who were praying at the Hebron mosque. Israelis pulled out of much of Hebron in early 1997 but Israeli settlers and troops remained in the centre of the town.

SOURCE K

Statement by the Civil Rights and Peace Movement in 1988:

Two peoples live in the Land of Israel – the Jewish people and the Palestinian–Arab people. Both have rights to this land. Therefore, the alternatives are clear: either compromise or endless war. The Jewish settlements are an obstacle to peace; the establishment of new settlements and the expansion of existing ones must be opposed.

SOURCE L

Statement by the Tehiya Party, 1988:

The exclusive and eternal right to the Land of Israel lies with the Jewish people. We will oppose all forms of compromise over the Land of Israel. The essence of the conflict is the desire of the Arabs to destroy the state of Israel. Israel's policy must be one of deterrence together with the strengthening of its arms arsenal. The expansion of Jewish settlements is not an obstacle to peace but, rather, the best guarantee for peace. The more settlements are created, the more the dream of a Palestinian state will fade.

SOURCE J

A Palestinian protester throws a gas canister back at Israeli soldiers during demonstrations after the Hebron massacre. Hebron is often the source of tension between settlers and Palestinians.

>> Activity

Look at Sources K and L. What differences are there between these two statements by Israelis? Using information from throughout this unit explain why Israelis hold very contrasting views about how Israel should be run.

Israel and the superpowers

After 1945 international politics were dominated by hostility between the superpowers — the USA and the Soviet Union. Historians call this conflict the 'Cold War'. In 1948 both superpowers supported the creation of Israel. In return, Israel tried to keep on friendly terms with both the USA and the Soviet Union. This neutrality continued until the Korean War started in 1950. Israel gave full support for the USA in its war against communism. A grateful US government promised to stand by Israel in the event of any attack. Israel and the USA signed a treaty of friendship in October 1951.

American influence over Israel was seen in the wars of 1956, 1967 and 1973. During the Suez crisis of 1956, Israel attacked Egypt, together with French and British forces. The Americans were not consulted and the US President, Eisenhower, was very angry at the Israeli action. The Israeli army successfully seized the Egyptian Sinai Desert but the American government insisted that the Israelis should withdraw. Over 10 years later, in June 1967, Israel went to war against Egypt, Syria and Jordan.

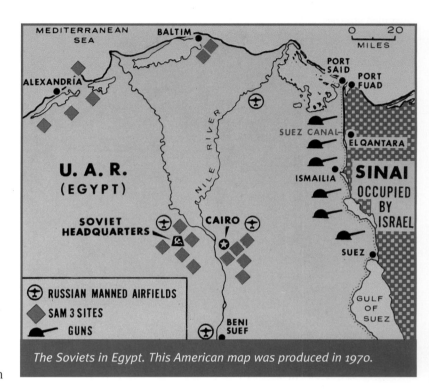

The Soviets in Egypt. This American map was produced in 1970.

In July 1983, the US Marine headquarters in Beirut was destroyed by a suicide bomber and hundreds of American soldiers were killed.

Having learned the lesson of 1956, the Israelis only attacked when sure of the support of the Americans. In October 1973 Israelis were shocked when the Egyptians launched a surprise attack. The Americans airlifted emergency supplies of arms to Israel to enable a successful counter-attack.

The heyday of Soviet influence

The Soviet Union was the world's leading communist country from 1917 to 1991. There was little sympathy for communist ideas in the Arab world. However, the need for arms drove the enemies of Israel towards friendly relations with Moscow. In 1955 the Soviet ally, Czechoslovakia supplied Egypt with weapons: everyone knew that the Soviet Union was behind this deal. The level of Soviet support for Arab states grew during the 1960s, particularly after 1967. By far the greatest support went to Egypt. In return for huge gifts of weaponry Soviet naval ships used Egyptian ports, and Soviet reconnaissance planes flew from Cairo airport.

President Clinton of the United States brought Yitzhak Rabin and Yasser Arafat together for a historic handshake after the signing of the Israeli–PLO peace accord at the White House on 13 September 1993. Arafat extended his hand first, while Rabin needed some encouragement from Clinton to shake hands.

The collapse of Soviet power and influence

Despite their Soviet weapons the Arab states were defeated in the wars of 1967 and 1973. This inevitably raised questions about the value of Soviet help. The Egyptian leader, Anwar Sadat expelled Soviet advisers from his country in 1972 and moved closer to the USA in the following years. The Americans used their new relationship with Egypt to bring about a peace deal between Israel and Egypt. The American president, Jimmy Carter brought Sadat and the Israeli leader, Begin, together in 1978 at Camp David in the USA, where they agreed the details of a peace treaty.

In 1985 a new reforming leader, Mikhail Gorbachev came to power in the Soviet Union. He looked for compromise with the USA and the Cold War came to an end. In 1991 the Soviet Union disintegrated into a number of smaller states (the most important of which was Russia). With the end of the Cold War and the collapse of the Soviet Union, the USA was the only remaining superpower. As a result American power to influence events in the Middle East increased.

In the 1990s the US government was giving at least $3 billion annually to the government of Israel. This was about one-quarter of all the aid that the USA gave worldwide. In return for this generous support the American government expected the Israeli government to follow American advice. However, the Americans were not always able to get their own way with Israel.

After 1988 the Americans tried to persuade the Israelis to negotiate with the Palestinians. This led to the Madrid peace conference in 1991. In 1992 President Bush told the Israelis to stop expanding Jewish settlements in the West Bank but the Israeli government refused to change its policy.

American pressure did eventually lead to the agreement of 1993. Bill Clinton was elected US president in 1992. He was keen to bring about peace in the Middle East. He was also a very strong supporter of Israel. In 1992 he said: 'Like America, Israel is a strong democracy, a symbol of freedom, an oasis of liberty, a home to the oppressed and persecuted. If I ever let Israel down, God would never forgive me.' Significantly, the 1993 peace deal between the PLO and the Israeli government was signed in Washington and President Bill Clinton forced the Israeli prime minister, Yitzhak Rabin, to shake hands with Yasser Arafat. After Rabin's death in 1996, Binyamin Netanyahu came to power. Clinton found it difficult to force Netanyahu to compromise with the Palestinians.

Discussion point

> Which of the two superpowers has been more successful in influencing events in the Middle East since 1948?

The Intifada and the 1993 peace agreement

The Arab–Israeli conflict was transformed in 1993. The Israeli prime minister, Yitzhak Rabin, signed an historic peace treaty with Yasser Arafat, of the PLO.

What were the causes and impact of the 1993 peace accord?

The Intifada

In December 1987 the Palestinians of the West Bank and the Gaza Strip began an uprising against Israeli rule. For over five years, thousands of young Palestinians confronted Israeli troops with stones and petrol bombs. This became known as the *Intifada* (meaning in Arabic 'shaking off'). The Israeli government tried to smash the Intifada by force. Many demonstrators were shot dead. Instructions from the Israeli chief of staff, Rafael Eitan, stated that anyone found breaking the curfew could be beaten before questions were asked. In five years over a thousand Palestinian demonstrators were killed by Israeli troops. In addition, several hundred Palestinians were killed by other Palestinians as suspected informers. The Israelis regularly sealed off Palestinian areas and placed people under curfew, forcing them to stay indoors. Soldiers were allowed to shoot dead anyone resisting arrest during the curfew. One leading Israeli critic, the former foreign minister Abba Eban, said: 'This meant that someone on the way to see a doctor would be risking his life.'

The street fighting was dominated by young Palestinians. Of all the people killed during the Intifada, 23 per cent were aged under 16. Schools and colleges were seen as centres of Palestinian agitation. The Israeli government responded by closing down the Palestinian school system for two years between 1988 and 1990. Palestinian universities were closed for four years. The shootings, the closures and the curfews did not stop the Intifada.

SOURCE A

These brightly dressed, hooded figures are the shababs – the resistance fighters who controlled the refugee camps during the Intifada.

> Look at the following interpretations of the Intifada. What differences are there between the two sources?

> How many different reasons can you think of to explain these different interpretations?

SOURCE B

Edward Said is a leading Palestinian–American historian and writer. He was born in Jerusalem but his family fled in 1948 and he settled in the USA. He wrote this account in 1992.

Conditions in the occupied territories

Jabalya Camp in Gaza is the most appalling place I have ever seen. There is no sewage system, the stench tears at your gut, and everywhere you look you see masses of people falling over each other, poorly dressed, glumly making their way from one seemingly hopeless task to the other. The Gaza Strip is made up of several towns, of refugee camps and, most offensive, of a number of affluent-looking Israeli settlements, whose spacious lawns and swimming pools are far removed in appearance from the squalor all around.

The events of the Intifada

Since the Intifada began in late 1987 until the end of June 1991, 983 have been killed by the Israeli military (that is three times the number of blacks killed by South African troops under apartheid during the same length of time); more than 120,000 wounded and beaten, and 15,000 prisoners, most of them without benefit of a trial. More than 1,882 houses have been punitively [as a punishment] demolished. Many schools and universities were closed, so determined has Israel been to criminalize [make criminal] Palestinian education. Literally thousands of days of total twenty-four-hour curfew confined almost two million unarmed and essentially defenceless civilians to their houses.

SOURCE C

Martin Gilbert is a leading British historian. He is Jewish and he is very sympathetic towards Israel. He teaches in Oxford, but he also has a house in Jerusalem. He wrote this account in 1993.

Conditions in the occupied territories

Despite their desire for independence, and dislike of Israeli occupation, the Palestinians living in the West Bank and Gaza benefited from the general social and economic policies of Israel. Before 1967 there were no universities; six were established after 1967.

Some improvements since the Israeli occupation

	Before 1967	After 1989
Clinics and hospitals	113	378
Mother and child centres	23	135
Villages with mains water	12	200
Malaria	Still a problem	Eliminated
Infant deaths per 1,000 births	86	20.4
School teachers	5,316	17,373
Teacher training colleges	0	5
Vocational colleges	0	14

The events of the Intifada

On 9 December 1987 an uprising, known as the Intifada, began in Gaza and spread throughout the Arab-populated areas of the West Bank. Israeli soldiers were attacked, mostly with rocks, but increasingly with knives, petrol bombs and even grenades. Many Arab villages sought to block the entry of Israeli soldiers, and Arab schoolchildren were encouraged by their elders to hurl stones and abuse. The Israeli army sought to regain control by the use of tear gas, rubber and plastic bullets and (when under extreme provocation) live ammunition. Excesses took place, and several Israeli soldiers were found guilty by Israeli courts for abuse of their powers. In 1991, stabbings of Jews became more frequent in Jewish urban areas. So too did the murder and maiming of Arabs by their fellow-Arabs, accused of 'collaboration with the authorities'.

The consequences of the Intifada

Worldwide opinion

The sight of stone-throwing young Palestinians confronting well-armed Israeli troops won worldwide admiration. In the past Israel had often seemed to be a brave underdog, surrounded by great numbers of Arab enemies. During the Intifada many people saw the Palestinians as the underdogs and the Israelis as brutal oppressors. Even the American government, the greatest supporter of Israel, became concerned and argued that the Israelis must compromise with the Palestinians.

SOURCE D

American frustration was expressed by George Shultz, the American Secretary of State in September 1988:

The status quo between the Arabs and the Israelis does not work. It is not viable. It is dangerous. Israel's security is paramount, but Palestinian political rights must also be recognised and addressed. The principle must be land for peace, and negotiation between Israel and the Palestinians.

The end of the Jordanian solution

Before 1967 the West Bank had been controlled by Jordan. In the 1970s and for much of the 1980s Israelis and Americans had talked about the possibility of a 'Jordanian' future for the Palestinians of the West Bank. By this they meant that the West Bank would not be allowed to become an independent Palestinian state but would be re-united with Jordan, under King Hussein. One result of the Intifada was that Hussein gave up claims to the West Bank in July 1988. This was a challenge to Israel and the USA — they could no longer talk about a Jordanian solution. If they wanted peace they must talk to the PLO, the only serious representative of the Palestinian people.

SOURCE E

The Palestinians had to be involved in the solution of the Palestinian problem. So we responded to that. We realised that these people want the responsibility of shaping the future in their own hands. They want to represent themselves.

King Hussein speaking in 1990

The PLO and the Intifada

The Intifada was a godsend for Yasser Arafat and the PLO. Since leaving Lebanon in 1982 the PLO had been trying unsuccessfully to put pressure on Israel. The Intifada had not been planned by the PLO but it proved very useful to them as a way of gaining support for the Palestinian cause. Arafat saw this as an opportunity to establish a Palestinian state in the West Bank and Gaza. To do this he knew he needed American support. In December 1988 Arafat announced that he was ready to make a number of important concessions required by the Americans.

The rise of Hamas

Not all the street fighters of the Intifada supported the PLO. Some Palestinians turned to a new grouping known as Hamas, that was founded in 1988. This was a fundamentalist Islamic organisation that rejected the idea of any compromise with Israel. It successfully organised community self-help in Gaza and the West Bank. Hamas was much more committed to strict Islamic traditions than the PLO. Hamas, for example, forced women in Gaza to wear head-scarves. While the PLO moved away from the use of violence Hamas members remained ready to kill in the struggle with Israel. Hamas carried out regular attacks on Israeli soldiers and civilians. Both the PLO and the Israeli government were worried by the rise of Hamas. In 1989 the Israeli government arrested the Hamas leader, Shaikh Ahmad Yasin. He was released from prison in 1997.

SOURCE F

Members of Hamas study Islamic scripture with their weapons by their sides.

SOURCE G

In August 1988 Hamas published its Charter, a statement of its core beliefs:

Hamas is working to unfurl the banner of Allah over every inch of Palestine. The only solution to the Palestinian problem is *jihad*. All peace conferences and proposals are no more than a waste of time. Those who die fighting against the Zionists will be martyrs.

The Gulf War

In 1990 Iraq, led by Saddam Hussein, invaded the small oil-rich state of Kuwait. Many Palestinians lived in Kuwait. With the backing of the United Nations, the USA organised a coalition army to throw the Iraqis out of Kuwait. This action was supported by many Arab states, including wealthy oil states such as Saudi Arabia. In contrast, Yasser Arafat refused to condemn Saddam Hussein. Many ordinary Palestinians supported Hussein because he often criticised Israel. The American-led coalition army launched a counter-attack in January 1991. During the fighting, Arafat visited Iraq and expressed support for Saddam Hussein.

SOURCE I

Palestinians expelled from Kuwait were forced to live in makeshift camps in bordering countries.

By the end of February 1991, the Iraqis had been driven from Kuwait. During the fighting the Iraqis had fired missiles at Israel. Once the war was over the Palestinians of Kuwait were punished for supporting Saddam Hussein. Most of the 400,000 Palestinians who had lived in Kuwait were expelled after the war. Palestinians suspected of collaborating with Iraq were imprisoned. Rich Gulf states, like Saudi Arabia, were unhappy with Arafat's actions. The Gulf states stopped financing the PLO and many other Palestinian organisations. The war left the PLO isolated and desperately short of money. This added to the pressure on Arafat to do a deal with Israel.

SOURCE H

Part of the American-led coalition army which was formed to throw the invading Iraqis out of Kuwait in 1991.

SOURCE J

President Bush with the Israeli prime minister, Yitzhak Shamir, in Madrid, October 1991. Bush put pressure on Shamir to compromise with the Palestinians.

American influence

The end of the Cold War and victory in the Gulf War strengthened the power of the Americans. The American Secretary of State, James Baker, was in charge of American foreign policy from 1989 to 1992 and he was keen to achieve peace in the Middle East. Baker worked for President Bush, who was prepared to get tough with the Israeli government. Bush and Baker put pressure on the hardline Israeli prime minister, Yitzhak Shamir, to start talking to the PLO. The message from the Americans was that unless progress was made, American financial support might be reduced. Shamir finally agreed to peace talks with Palestinians but not with official members of the PLO leadership. The peace conference was held in Madrid, Spain and began in October 1991.

June 1992 – a change of government in Israel

The Madrid talks made little progress. The Israelis refused to make any concessions to the Palestinians. Shamir later said that his plan was to drag the talks out for up to 10 years. The situation changed dramatically in June 1992 when Shamir lost the Israeli general election. The new Israeli prime minister was the Labour Party leader, Yitzhak Rabin. Unlike Shamir, Rabin was prepared to make a deal with the Palestinians. At first Rabin hoped to be able to come to an agreement with local Palestinians, cutting out the PLO leaders. This strategy failed – local Palestinians refused to cut their links with Arafat. Rabin soon decided that he would have to talk to Arafat.

The rise of Hamas encouraged both the PLO and the Israeli government to make peace. There was an upsurge of Hamas attacks on Israeli targets in December 1992. Arafat was afraid that unless he could achieve a peace treaty with Israel, more and more Palestinians would desert the PLO and support Hamas. Rabin did not like Arafat but he was convinced that Hamas was worse than the PLO. Like Arafat, he was concerned at the idea that Hamas might replace the PLO as the main representative of the Palestinian people.

Breakthrough in Oslo

While the Madrid talks continued in public, more substantial, secret negotiations took place in Oslo, Norway between the Israeli government and the PLO. Agreement was reached on 30 August 1993 in Oslo and two weeks later, on 13 September, Rabin and Arafat came to an agreement in Washington. (The peace deal is often referred to as the Oslo Accord because the detail was worked out in Norway.)

SOURCE K

September 1993 – Declaration of Principles

The Government of the State of Israel and the PLO, representing the Palestinian people, agree that it is time to put an end to decades of confrontation and conflict, recognise their mutual legitimate and political rights, and strive to live in peaceful coexistence and mutual dignity and security and achieve a just, lasting and comprehensive peace settlement and historic reconciliation.

The agreement was not a final settlement. It established a Palestinian Authority which would give Palestinians control over much of daily life in Gaza and the West Bank but put off long-term decisions about difficult issues, such as Jewish settlements and the future of Jerusalem. An armed Palestinian police force was established. The Israelis promised to withdraw the army from most populated areas but the Israeli army remained in the territories and was responsible for the security of Jewish settlers. The agreement began to be put into effect in May 1994. In that year, Arafat, Rabin and Shimon Peres, the Israeli foreign minister, jointly won the Nobel Prize for Peace.

In July 1994 Arafat and the PLO leadership left Tunisia and moved to the Gaza Strip. A Palestinian Authority, headed by Arafat, took control of much of daily life in Gaza and in the West Bank town of Jericho. After further negotiations, Arafat and Rabin signed a new agreement in September 1995 which extended the power of the Palestinian Authority beyond Jericho to much of the rest of the West Bank. The details were again negotiated at Oslo and the agreement was known as 'Oslo II'. In January 1996 elections were held and Arafat became president of the Palestinian Authority.

After the signing of the agreement with the PLO in 1993, the Israeli government began peace negotiations with Jordan. This led to a formal peace treaty between the two countries in July 1994. The Americans and the Israelis hoped that the next stage would be peace between Israel and Syria but this proved much more difficult to bring about. From the Israeli point of view there was no longer any danger of attack from Egypt or Jordan, but Lebanon and Syria remained areas of potential threat.

SOURCE L

Arafat, Rabin and Peres receive their awards at the Nobel Prize ceremony.

Palestinian response to the Oslo Accord

A majority of Palestinians in Gaza and the West Bank welcomed the agreements with Israel. A large minority, including Hamas and some factions within the PLO, objected, for a number of reasons, to the way that Arafat had made concessions.

> The agreement did not remove the Jewish settlements from the West Bank.

> Israeli settlers were not placed under the authority of the new Palestinian administration.

> Arab East Jerusalem was excluded from the agreement.

> Israeli armed forces remained present in the Palestinian territories.

> It offered nothing to Palestinians living in refugee camps in Lebanon, Jordan or Syria.

SOURCE M

An elderly Palestinian man who had been expelled from his own village in 1950 made this comment on the news of the agreement.

I feel like a man who has lost a million dollars and been given ten. But you see, I lost the million dollars a long time ago. So I will keep the ten. We cannot go on the way we are. I accept, I accept, I accept. After so many rejections, I accept. But, please, don't ask me how I feel.

SOURCE N

A leading member of Hamas criticised the agreement in 1995:

The Oslo Accord has made things worse for us. Israel continues its illegal occupation but this has now been accepted by the international community which thinks that peace has been achieved. This is untrue. Israel must be demolished by continuing struggle on the part of Muslims. The whole of Palestine is holy land to every Muslim in the world.

SOURCE O

A member of the PLO who was unhappy with the leadership of Arafat made this statement in late 1993:

Let us call the agreement by its real name: a Palestinian surrender. The PLO has ended the Intifada, even though Israel remains in occupation of the West Bank and Gaza. There is nothing in the document to suggest that Israel will give up its violence against Palestinians or compensate its victims. Israeli troops will redeploy, not totally withdraw. Israeli settlers will remain and live under different laws.

>> Activity

1   What was agreed at Oslo in 1993?

2   Why did the government of Israel sign a peace treaty with the PLO in 1993? In your answer you could mention:
> the Intifada
> the impact of Hamas
> the Gulf War
> American pressure
> the Israeli elections in June 1992.

3   Look at Sources M, N and O. These statements were made by three different Palestinians. What do they tell us about why some Palestinians were unhappy with the agreement?

The assassination of Rabin

The peace agreements upset many right-wing and religious Israelis. They saw the Oslo Accords as steps towards a completely independent Palestinian state in Gaza and the West Bank. The idea of abandoning the West Bank — the scene of many events in ancient Jewish history — appalled these people. The leaders of Likud and other right-wing groups did not believe PLO statements that they were renouncing violence and now accepted the existence of Israel — for them a Palestinian mini-state was the first step in a plot to destroy the whole of Israel. There were large, angry demonstrations against the government of Yitzhak Rabin.

SOURCE P

The Likud politician and former prime minister, Yitzhak Shamir criticised the Oslo Accord in 1994:

These developments bear within them the seeds of disaster for the Jewish state. For the first time ever, an Israeli government had consented to give away parts of the Land of Israel, thus helping to pave the way to the inevitable establishment of a Palestinian state in Judea, Samaria and Gaza. The lives of 130,000 settlers were put at risk by the new policy.

Extremists on both sides used violence to wreck the moves towards peace. A small number of Jews were ready to kill to stop Palestinian control of the West Bank. A Jewish settler, Baruch Goldstein, shot and killed 29 Palestinians at the historic mosque in the centre of Hebron in February 1994. He was overpowered and beaten to death by survivors. To some Jewish extremists, Goldstein was a martyr and his grave at Kiryat Arba, near Hebron, became a place of pilgrimage.

Palestinians were outraged by the Hebron massacre and Hamas planned revenge. Some Hamas members strapped explosives to their bodies and blew themselves up when they were close to a large number of Israelis. These suicide attacks often took place on public buses. In April 1994, two Hamas suicide bombers blew themselves up killing 12 Israelis. In October a suicide bomber in Tel Aviv killed 22 people. In January 1995 a further 21 Israelis were killed by another suicide bomb. These events were only the most spectacular examples of violence. Between the first Oslo Accord in September 1993 and January 1995, 345 people were killed in political violence.

On 4 November 1995 a Jewish extremist, Yigal Amir, shot dead the prime minister, Yitzhak Rabin. Amir was a keen supporter of the settler movement and saw Rabin as an enemy of the Jewish people. The assassination of Rabin was a terrible event for most Israelis. It revealed the divided nature of Israeli society. Rabin's foreign minister, Shimon Peres, took over as prime minister. The murder of Rabin was a real turning-point in Israeli history. If Rabin had remained alive, Labour would almost certainly have won the 1996 general election. Peres was less popular and he went on to lose the election.

SOURCE Q

King Hussein of Jordan addresses the mourners at the funeral of Yitzhak Rabin in November 1995.

SOURCE R

A UN soldier and civilians try to deal with the body of a victim of the Israeli attack on the UN base near Tyre.

The election of 1996

The position of Peres and the Labour Party was undermined by Hamas attacks. Suicide bomb attacks in February and March 1996 killed 59 people. This contributed to a feeling in Israel that the peace agreements were not working. In April 1996 Israeli troops invaded southern Lebanon. Half a million people became temporary refugees. Peres wanted to show that he could be tough by stopping the Islamic fighters of Hizbollah from Lebanon firing missiles at northern Israel. Before the Israeli forces withdrew, 150 people were killed; 94 Lebanese civilians were killed on 18 April when the Israelis fired on a United Nations base near Tyre. Despite his tough action Peres was unable to destroy the Hizbollah fighters and he finally agreed to a cease-fire.

In May 1996 the Labour government of Shimon Peres lost power in the Israeli general election to Likud, led by Binyamin Netanyahu. For the first time ever Israelis voted directly for their prime minister. Netanyahu was the winner, but the result was remarkably close – Peres got 1.47 million votes, Netanyahu received 1.50 million votes. To many outside observers the election seemed to threaten peace between Jews and Palestinians. Peres had intended to give Palestinians greater powers and, possibly, an independent Palestinian state on the West Bank and Gaza. Netanyahu opposed the idea of a separate Palestinian state. His government included hardliners, such as Ariel Sharon, the man behind the 1982 Lebanon invasion.

The new Likud government immediately expanded settlements in the West Bank, closed down Palestinian offices in Jerusalem and announced that there would be no concessions to Syria over the Golan Heights. For months Netanyahu blocked the plan, agreed at Oslo II, for the Israeli forces to pull out of most of Hebron. The Palestinians were angered by these developments. In September 1996 tension reached new heights when Israelis opened a tourist tunnel near the al-Aqsa Mosque in Jerusalem. This deeply offended Palestinians because they saw it as a threat to their holy places. Violence broke out in the town of Ramallah near Jerusalem, and soon spread across the West Bank and Gaza. In gun battles between the Palestinian police and the Israeli armed forces from 25 to 27 September 1996, 68 people were killed. Sporadic violence continued throughout 1997. In January 1997 Israeli forces finally pulled out of much, but not all, of Hebron. In March Netanyahu announced plans for a massive expansion of Jewish settlements in east Jerusalem. Hamas responded with a suicide bomb in July 1997 that killed 14 people.

>> Activity

Why did the agreements of 1993 and 1995 fail to bring peace to Israel?

Israel and the Palestinians since 1967

The Six Day War

In early 1967 the Egyptian leader, Nasser, threatened Israel with war. The Israelis responded by launching a surprise attack on Egypt on 5 June. This was the start of the Six Day War between Israel and several Arab states. Israeli planes rapidly destroyed the Egyptian airforce. Israeli ground forces seized territory from Egypt, Jordan and Syria. This occupied land included the Gaza Strip. east Jerusalem and the West Bank. Since 1967 the Israeli government has encouraged many Jews to move to new settlements in east Jerusalem and the West Bank. These settlements have been greatly resented by the Palestinian people.

The PLO

After the failure of the Arab armies in 1967, many Palestinians decided that neighbouring Arab states would never defeat Israel. They turned instead to the PLO (Palestine Liberation Organisation) and its leader, Yasser Arafat. After 1967 the PLO used a mixture of violence and diplomacy to try to win support from several countries; they were forced to leave Jordan in 1971 and Lebanon in 1982.

Yom Kippur

In October 1973 Egypt and Syria attacked Israel. The Israelis were taken completely by surprise and, at first, the Arab armies made rapid advances. Eventually, the Israelis fought back successfully and retook the land they had lost. Nevertheless, the War of Yom Kippur was a great shock to many Israelis. The 1973 war was planned by the Egyptian leader, Sadat. After the war Sadat tried to negotiate a peace settlement with the Israeli government. A peace settlement between Sadat and the Israeli prime minister, Begin, was eventually agreed in 1978. Peace with Egypt allowed Begin to invade Lebanon in 1982.

The Intifada and the 1993 peace deal

An uprising against the Israelis began in 1988 among young Palestinians of the Gaza Strip and the West Bank. Demonstrators threw rocks at the well-armed Israeli troops. This rebellion was known as the *Intifada*. The uprising won widespread support for the Palestinian people around the world. PLO leaders saw the Intifada as a chance to begin peace negotiations from a position of strength. In December 1988 Arafat finally publicly accepted the existence of Israel and rejected the use of terrorism. The USA put pressure on the Israeli government to make peace. At first the Israelis were reluctant to do a deal. In 1993 the PLO and the government of Israel finally agreed to end their hostility and sign a peace treaty. The PLO was given limited power in some areas of Gaza and the West Bank.

Index